The essential Nü METAL playlist

This publication is not authorised for sale in
the United States of America and / or Canada

WISE PUBLICATIONS
part of The Music Sales Group

London / New York / Paris / Sydney / Copenhagen / Berlin / Madrid / Tokyo

Published by
Wise Publications
8/9 Frith Street, London W1D 3JB, England.

Exclusive Distributors:
Music Sales Limited
Distribution Centre, Newmarket Road, Bury St Edmunds, Suffolk IP33 3YB, England.
Music Sales Pty Limited
120 Rothschild Avenue, Rosebery, NSW 2018, Australia.

Order No. AM980991
ISBN 1-84449-722-4
This book © Copyright 2005 by Wise Publications.

Compiled by Nick Crispin.
Music arranged by Matt Cowe and Arthur Dick.
Music processed by Paul Ewers Music Design.
Cover designed by Michael Bell Design.
Cover photograph courtesy of Mick Hutson/Redferns.
Printed in Great Britain.

Your Guarantee of Quality:
As publishers, we strive to produce every book to the highest commercial standards.
The music has been freshly engraved and the book has been carefully
designed to minimise awkward page turns and to make playing from it a real pleasure.
Particular care has been given to specifying acid-free, neutral-sized paper
made from pulps which have not been elemental chlorine bleached.
This pulp is from farmed sustainable forests and was produced with special regard for the environment.
Throughout, the printing and binding have been planned to ensure a sturdy,
attractive publication which should give years of enjoyment.
If your copy fails to meet our high standards, please inform us and we will gladly replace it.

www.musicsales.com

ALIVE P.O.D. 5

CHOP SUEY! SYSTEM OF A DOWN 12

COCHISE AUDIOSLAVE 21

CRAWLING LINKIN PARK 26

DEAD STAR MUSE 34

DISPOSABLE TEENS MARILYN MANSON 40

FALLING AWAY FROM ME KORN 52

GIRL'S NOT GREY AFI 46

I AM HATED SLIPKNOT 59

LAST RESORT PAPA ROACH 76

LOW FOO FIGHTERS 66

MEIN HERZ BRENNT RAMMSTEIN 83

NUMB LINKIN PARK 88

PARTY HARD ANDREW W.K. 100

RIGHT HERE IN MY ARMS HIM 94

SLITHER VELVET REVOLVER 105

TAKE A LOOK AROUND (THEME FROM "M:I-2")
LIMP BIZKIT 114

WAKE UP RAGE AGAINST THE MACHINE 124

GUITAR TABLATURE EXPLAINED 4

GUITAR TABLATURE EXPLAINED

Guitar music can be notated three different ways: on a musical stave, in tablature, and in rhythm slashes.

RHYTHM SLASHES are written above the stave. Strum chords in the rhythm indicated. Round noteheads indicate single notes.

THE MUSICAL STAVE shows pitches and rhythms and is divided by lines into bars. Pitches are named after the first seven letters of the alphabet.

TABLATURE graphically represents the guitar fingerboard. Each horizontal line represents a string, and each number represents a fret.

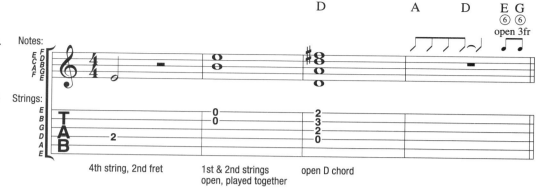

4th string, 2nd fret   1st & 2nd strings open, played together   open D chord

DEFINITIONS FOR SPECIAL GUITAR NOTATION

SEMI-TONE BEND: Strike the note and bend up a semi-tone (1/2 step).

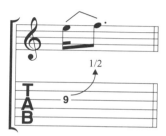

WHOLE-TONE BEND: Strike the note and bend up a whole-tone (whole step).

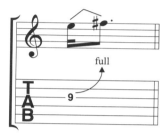

GRACE NOTE BEND: Strike the note and bend as indicated. Play the first note as quickly as possible.

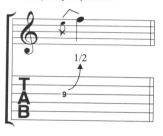

QUARTER-TONE BEND: Strike the note and bend up a 1/4 step.

BEND & RELEASE: Strike the note and bend up as indicated, then release back to the original note.

COMPOUND BEND & RELEASE: Strike the note and bend up and down in the rhythm indicated.

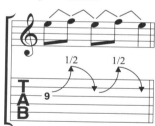

PRE-BEND: Bend the note as indicated, then strike it.

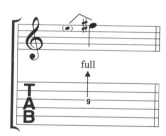

PRE-BEND & RELEASE: Bend the note as indicated. Strike it and release the note back to the original pitch.

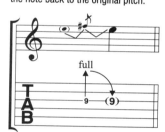

HAMMER-ON: Strike the first note with one finger, then sound the second note (on the same string) with another finger by fretting it without picking.

PULL-OFF: Place both fingers on the notes to be sounded, strike the first note and without picking, pull the finger off to sound the second note.

LEGATO SLIDE (GLISS): Strike the first note and then slide the same fret-hand finger up or down to the second note. The second note is not struck.

MUFFLED STRINGS: A percussive sound is produced by laying the fret hand across the string(s) without depressing, and striking them with the pick hand.

NATURAL HARMONIC: Strike the note while the fret-hand lightly touches the string directly over the fret indicated.

PICK SCRAPE: The edge of the pick is rubbed down (or up) the string, producing a scratchy sound.

PALM MUTING: The note is partially muted by the pick hand lightly touching the string(s) just before the bridge.

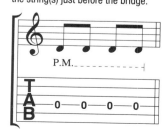

SHIFT SLIDE (GLISS & RESTRIKE): Same as legato slide, except the second note is struck.

NOTE: The speed of any bend is indicated by the music notation and tempo.

Alive

Words & Music by Marcos Curiel, Mark Daniels, Paul Sandoval & Noah Bernardo

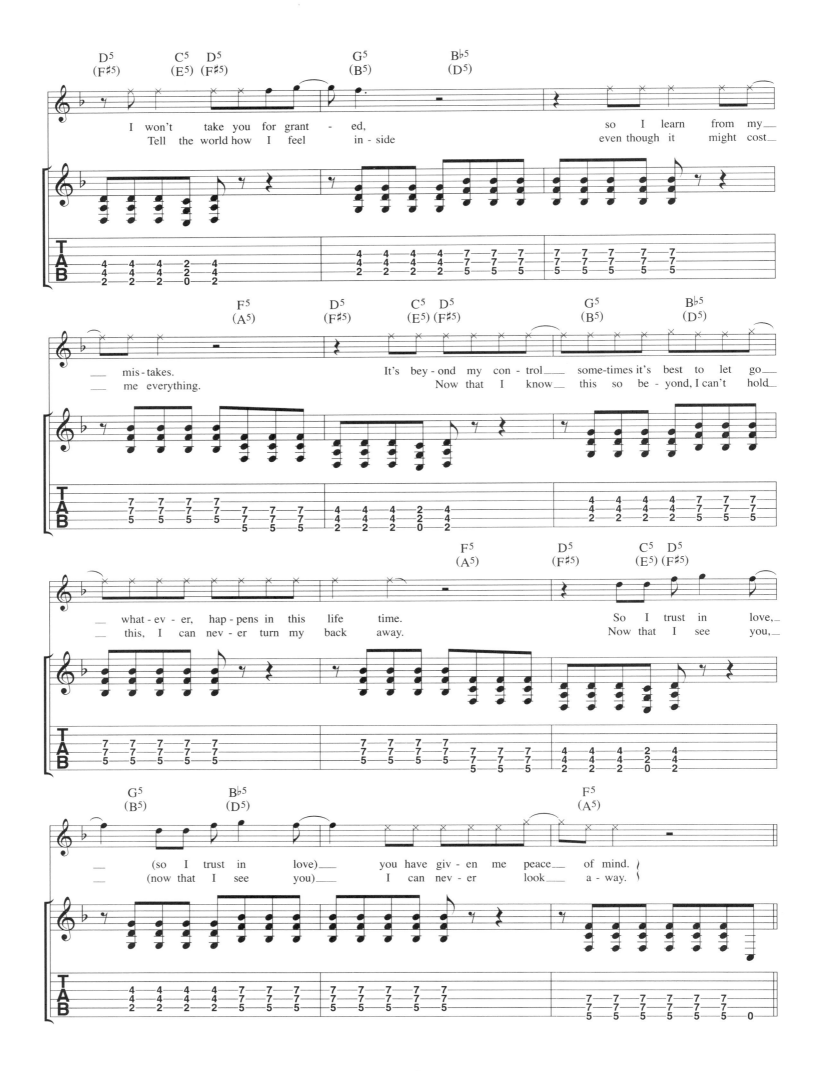

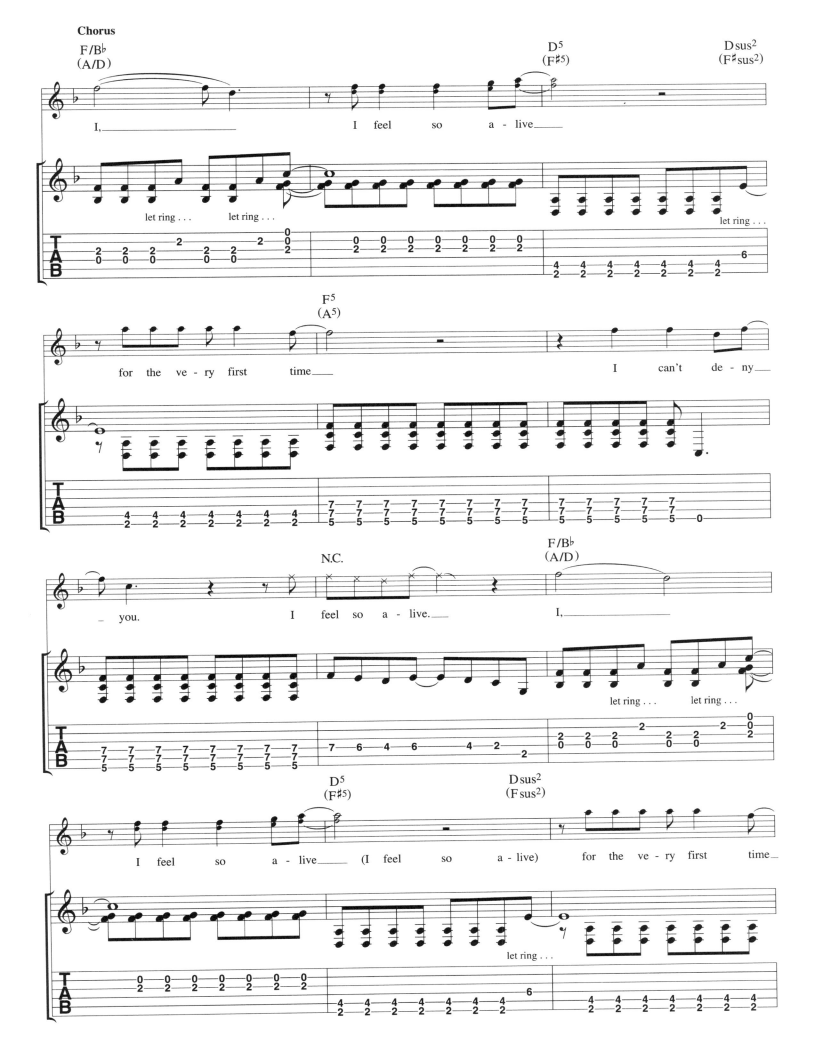

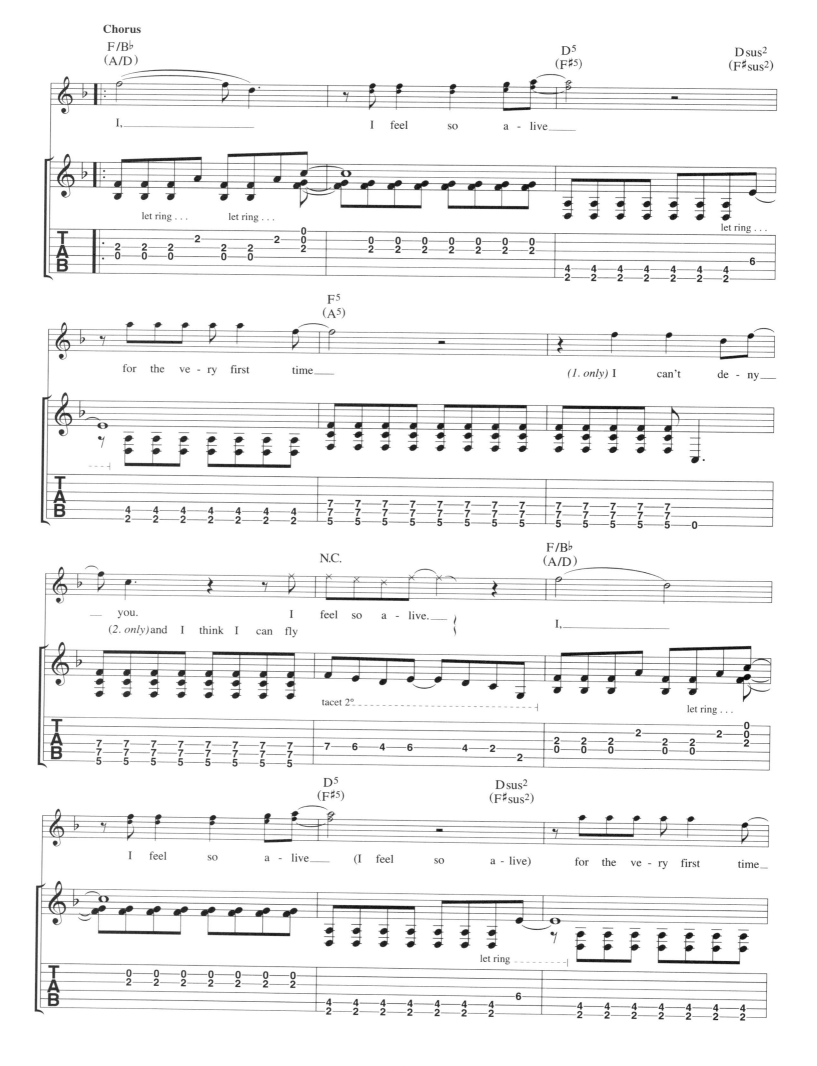

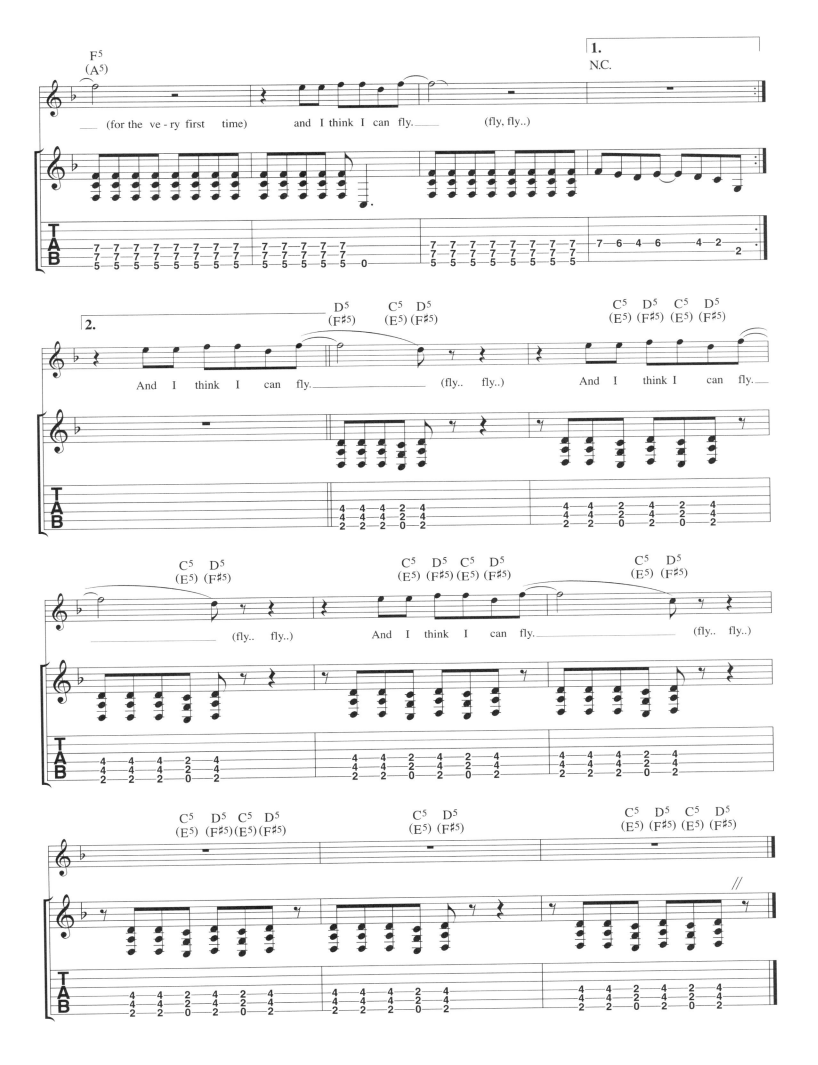

CHOP SUEY!

Words by Serj Tankian & Daron Malakian
Music by Daron Malakian

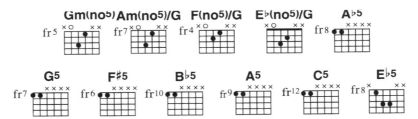

Tune gtr. Drop D tuning, down a tone:

⑥ = C   ③ = F
⑤ = G   ② = A
④ = C   ① = D

Intro (Acoustic riff)

** chords in brackets refer to standard tuning chord shapes/positions

* chords implied by harmony

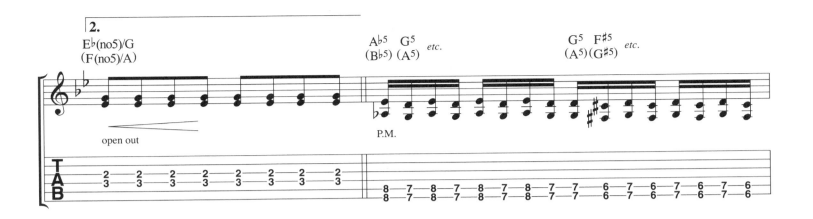

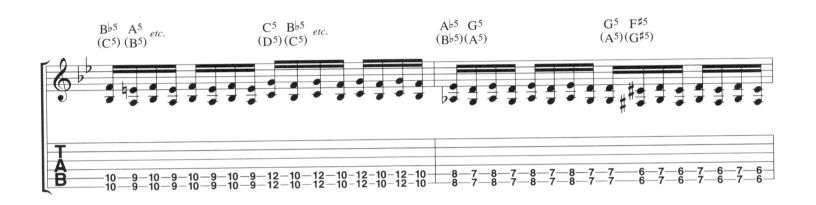

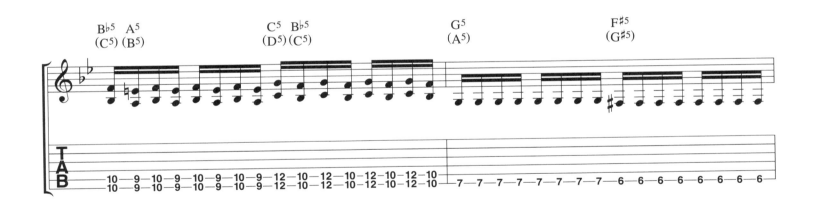

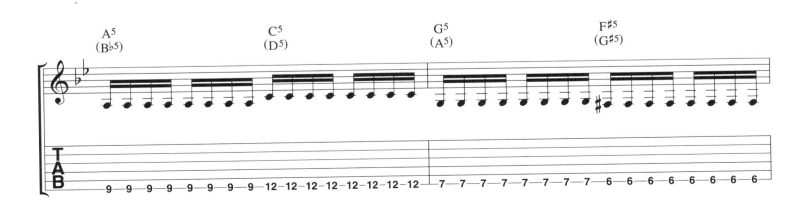

14

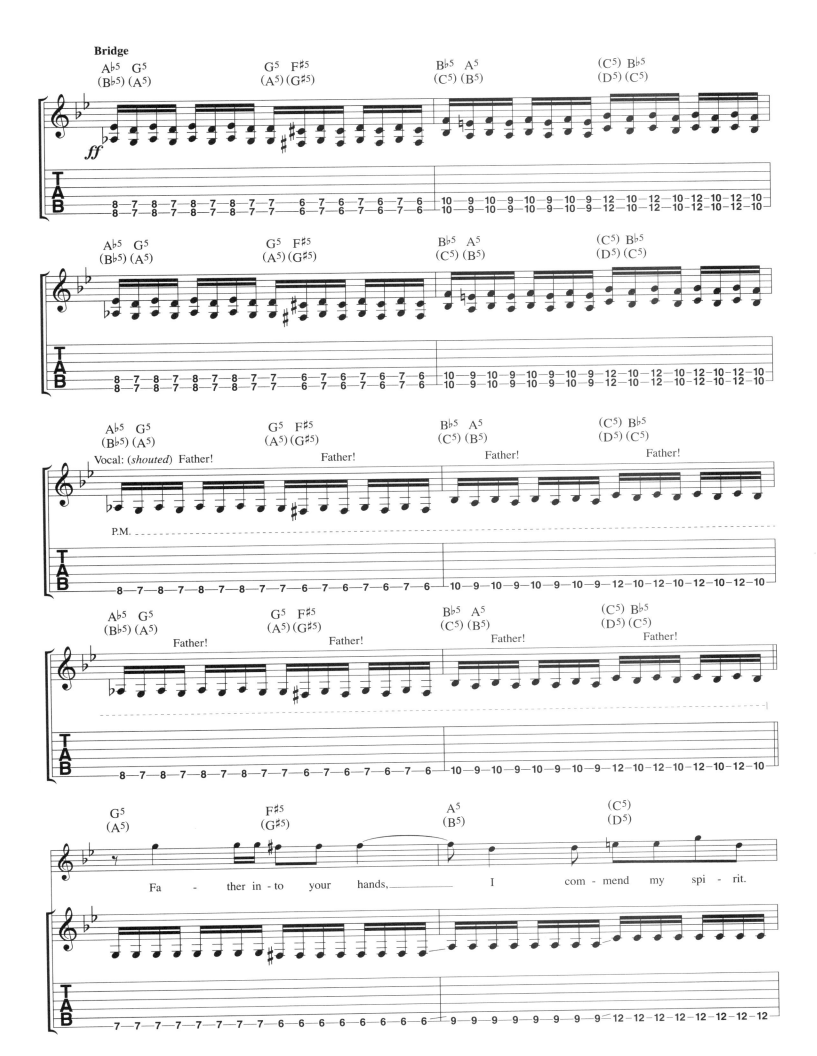

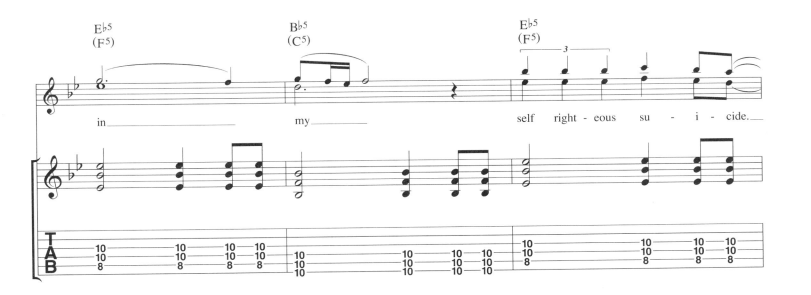

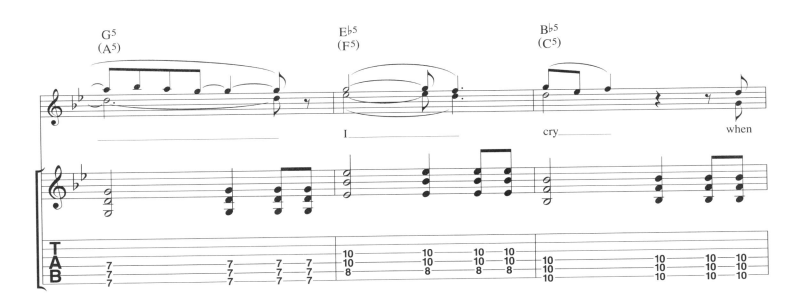

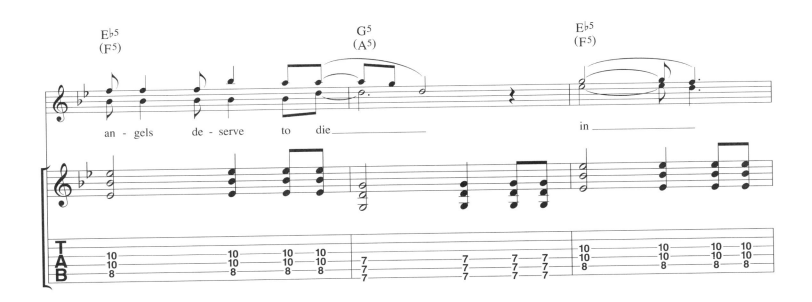

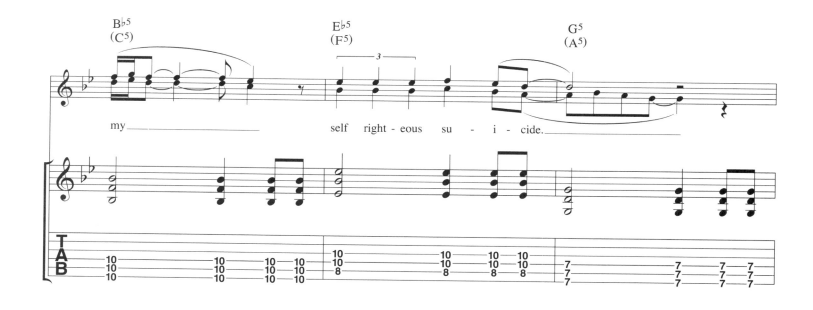

my _____ self right - eous su - i - cide. _____

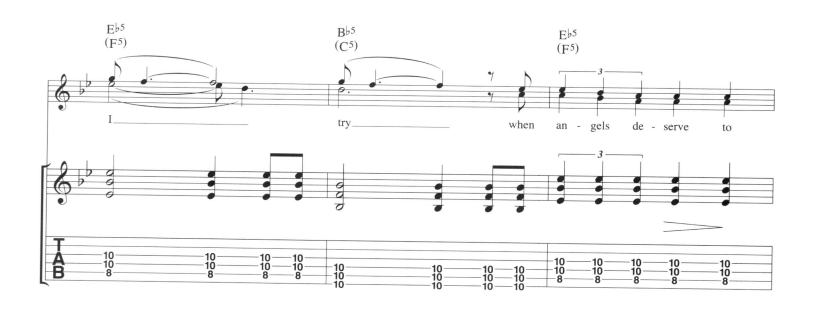

I _____ try _____ when an - gels de - serve to

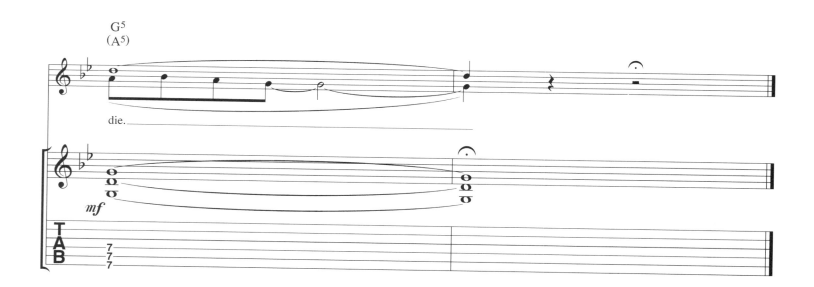

die. _____

COCHISE

words by chris cornell

music by chris cornell, tim commerford, tom morello & brad wilk

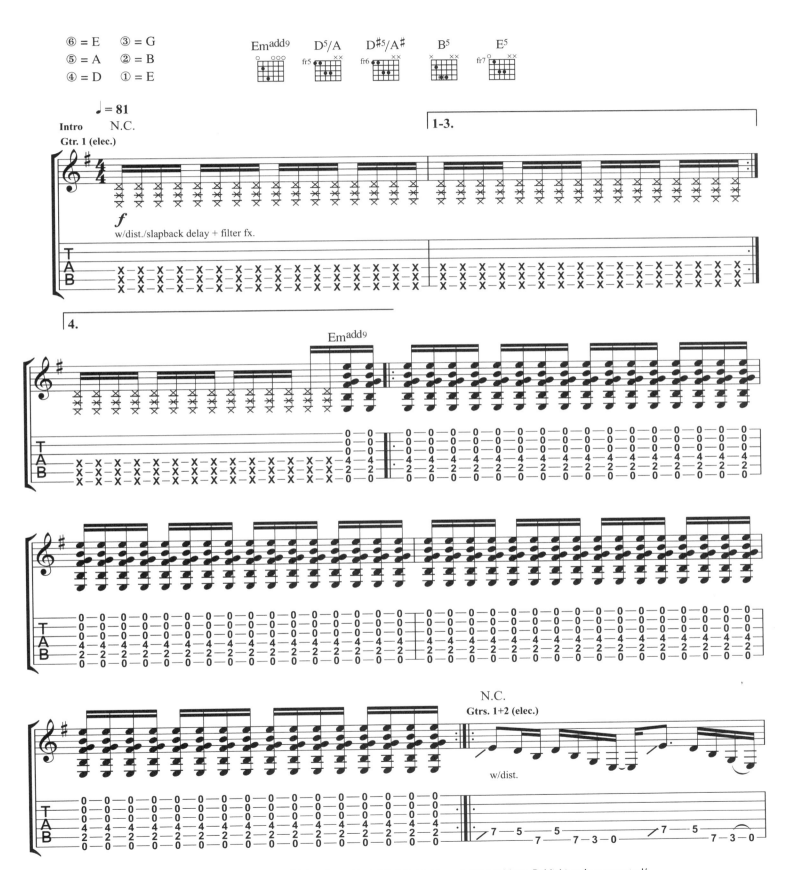

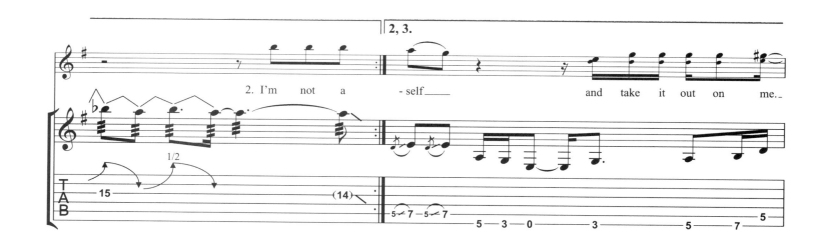

2. I'm not a - self____ and take it out on me.__

Go on and save your - self____ and take it out on me.

To Coda ⊕

Go on and save your - self____ and take it out on me,_____ yeah.

let ring

Bridge

B⁵

Drown____ if____ you want, and I'll see you at the bot - tom____ where you'll

CRAWLING

Words & Music by Chester Bennington, Mike Shinoda,
Rob Bourdon, Joseph Hahn & Brad Delson

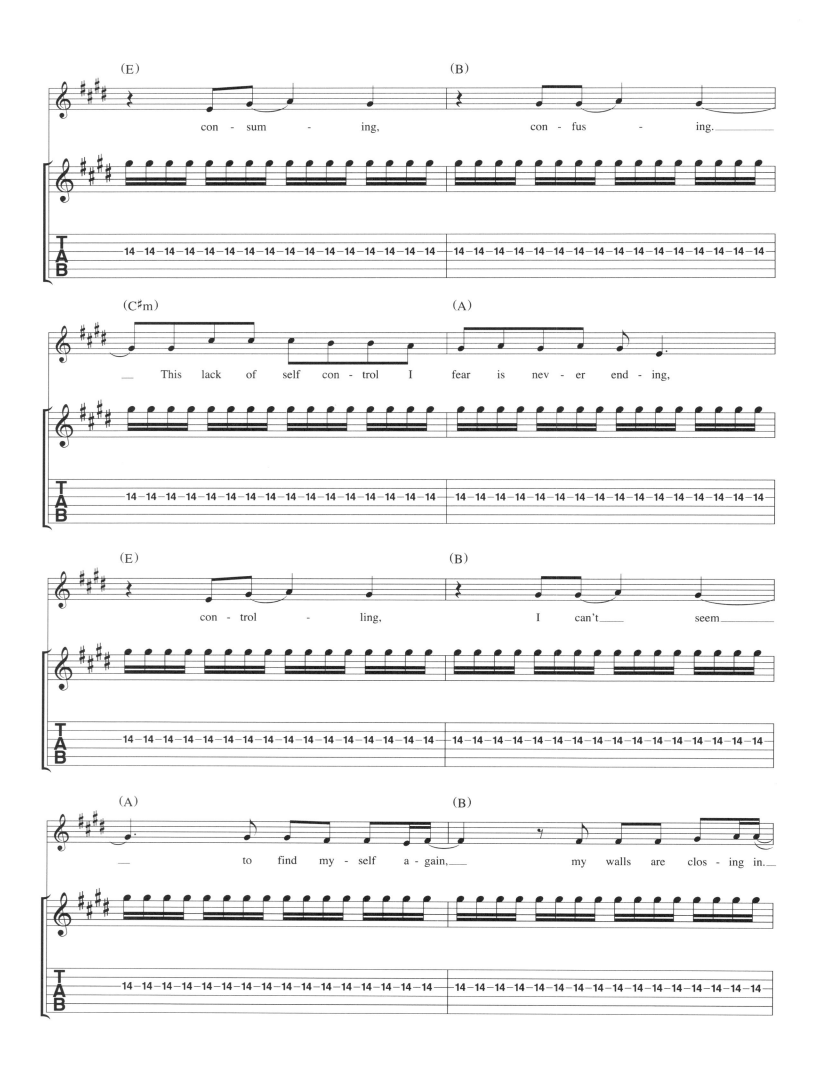

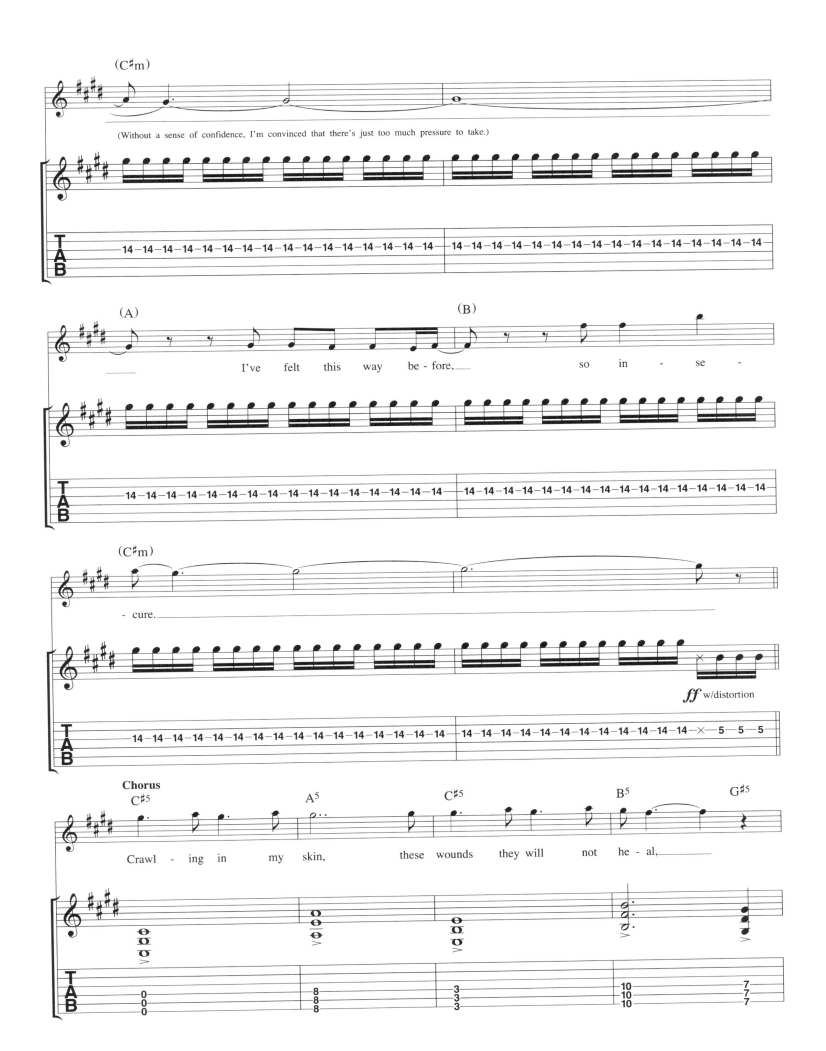

(C♯m)

(Without a sense of confidence, I'm convinced that there's just too much pressure to take.)

(A)

I've felt this way be - fore, so in - se -

(B)

(C♯m)

- cure.

ff w/distortion

Chorus

C♯5   A5   C♯5   B5   G♯5

Crawl - ing in my skin, these wounds they will not he - al,

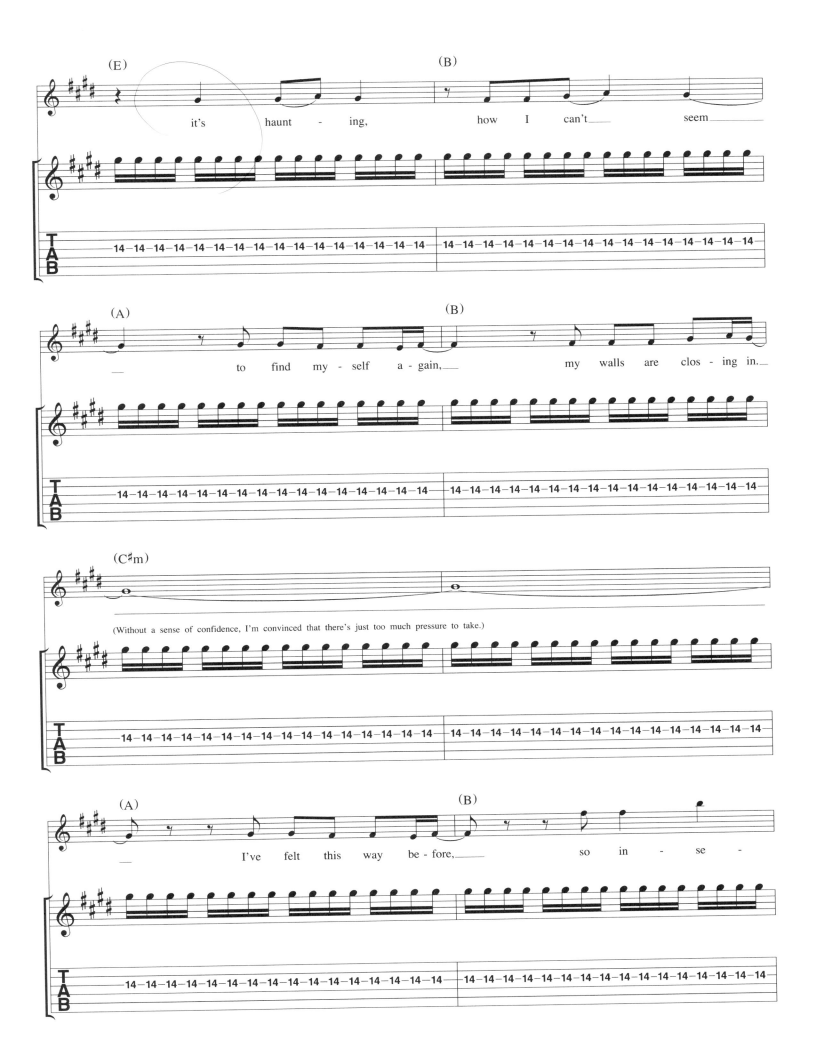

DEAD STAR

Words & Music by Matthew Bellamy

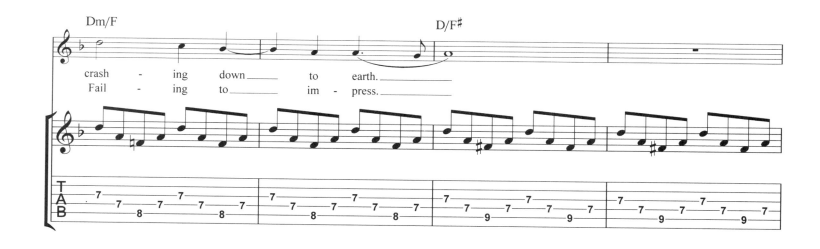

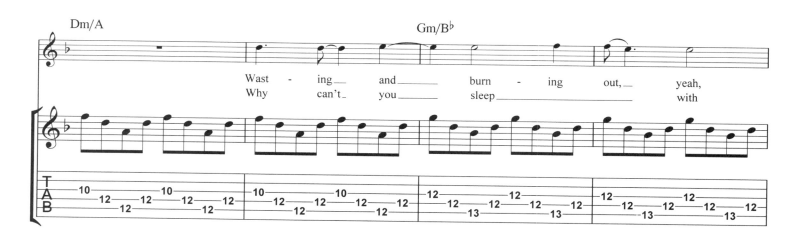

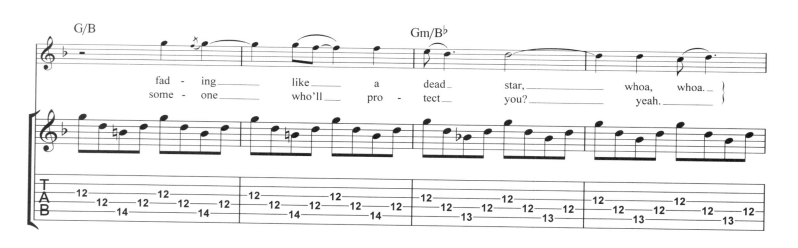

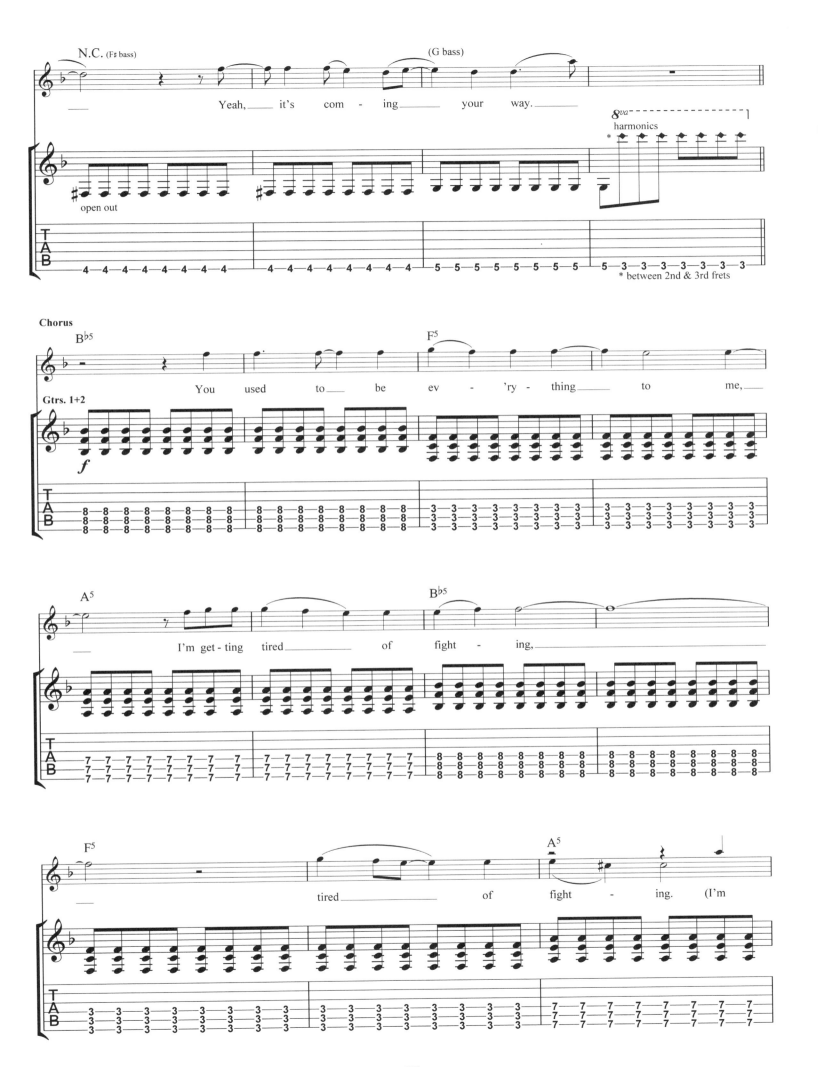

DISPOSABLE TEENS

words & music by Marilyn Manson,
John Lowery & Twiggy Ramirez

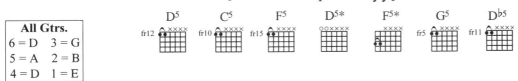

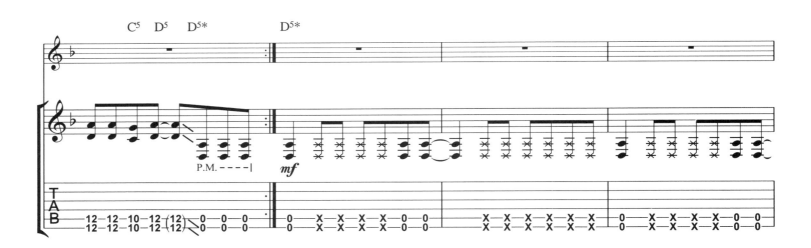

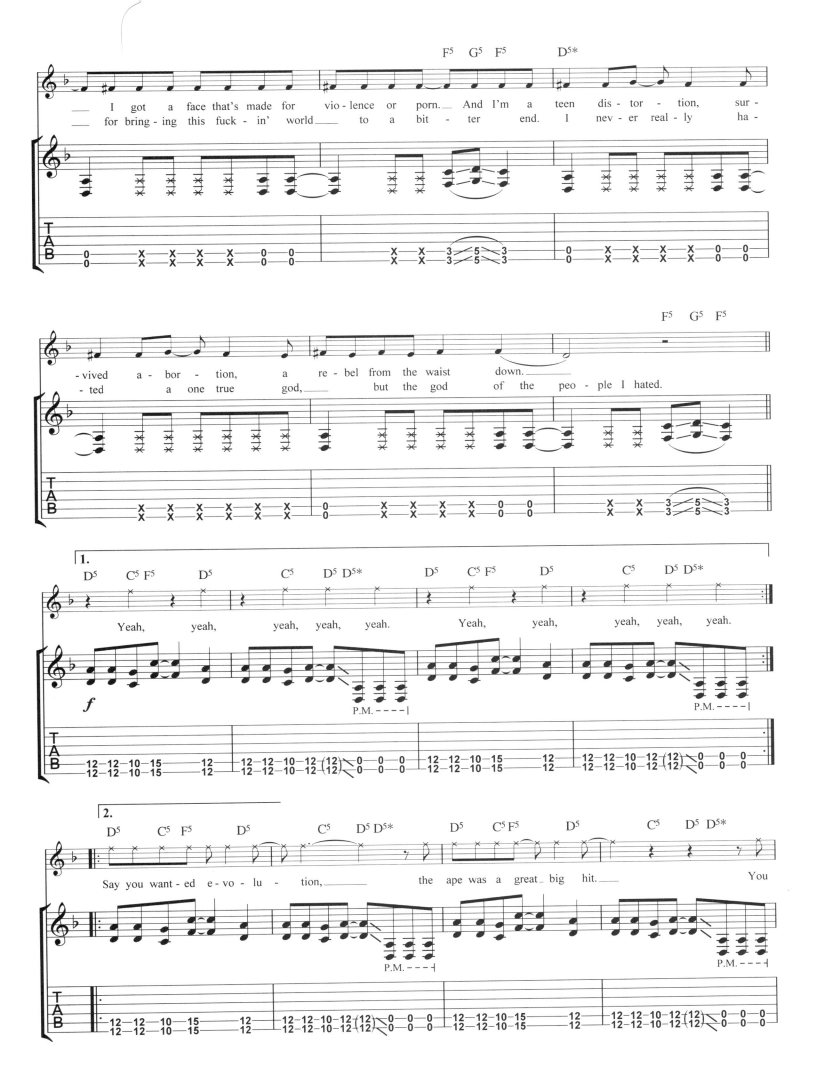

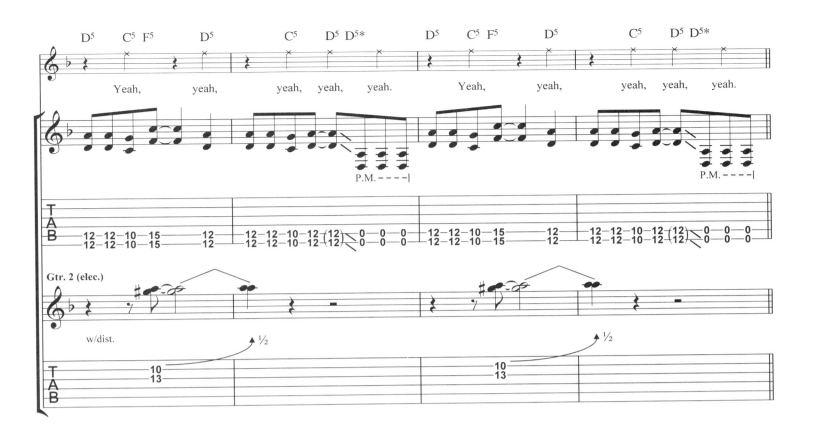

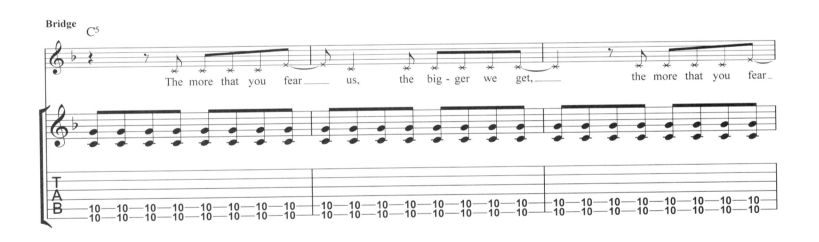

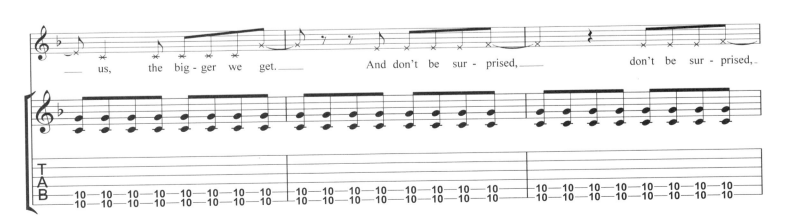

GIRL'S NOT GREY

Words & Music by David Marchand, Jade Puget,
Adam Carson & Hunter Burgan

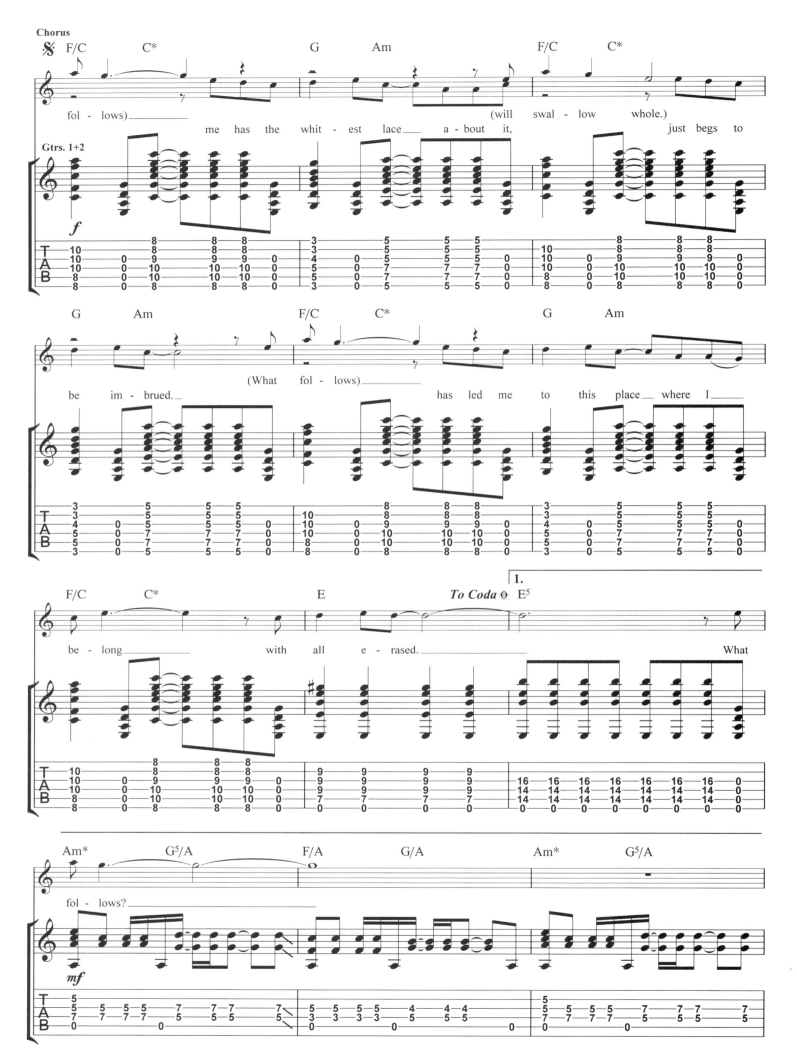

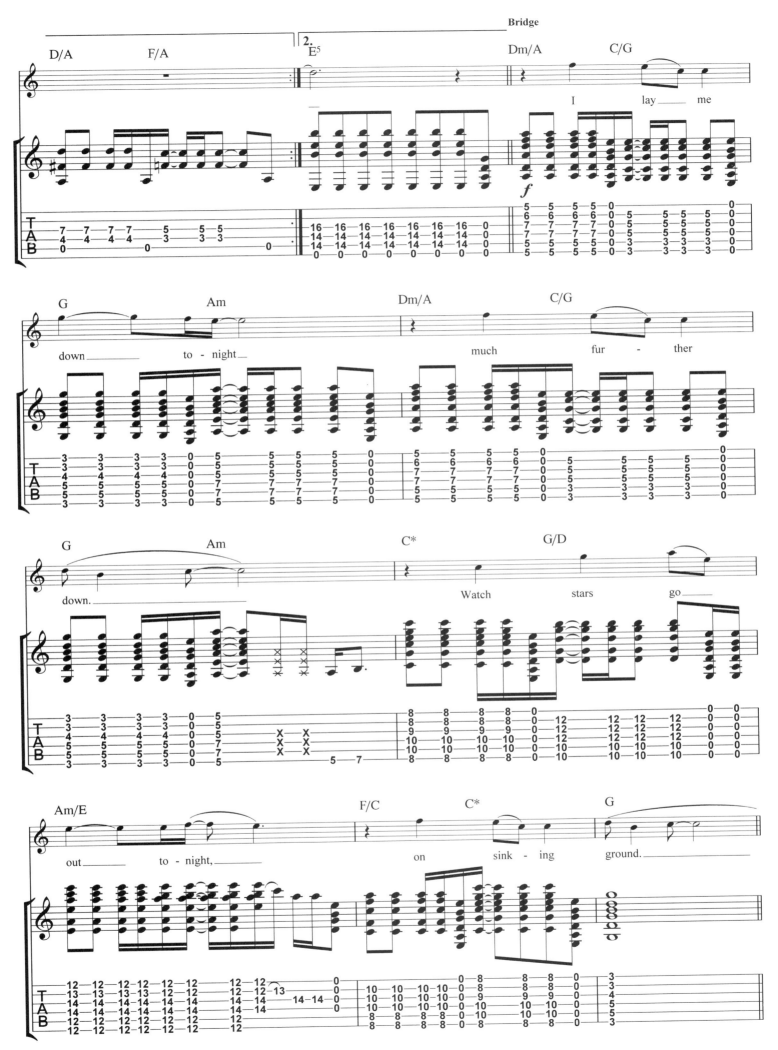

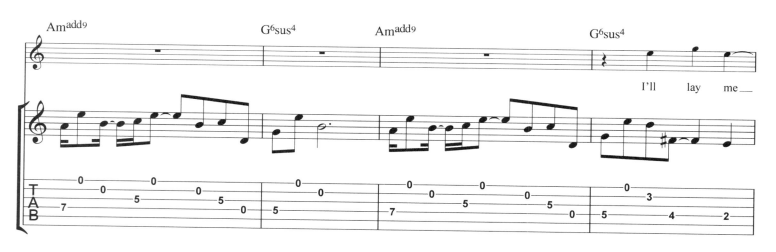

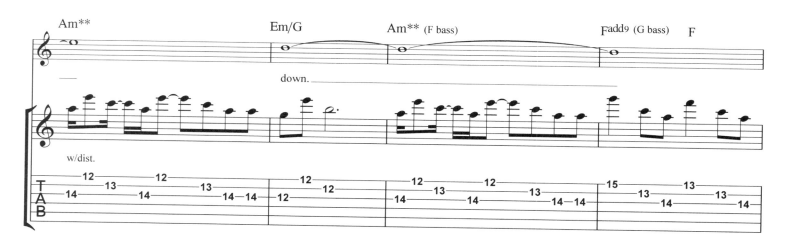

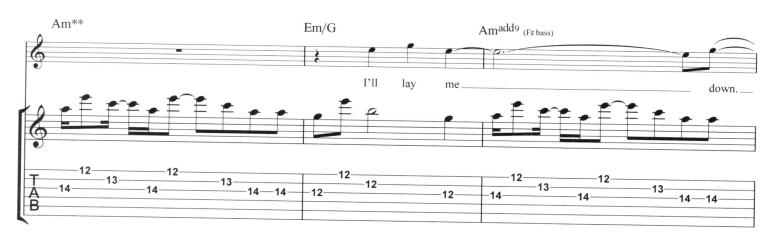

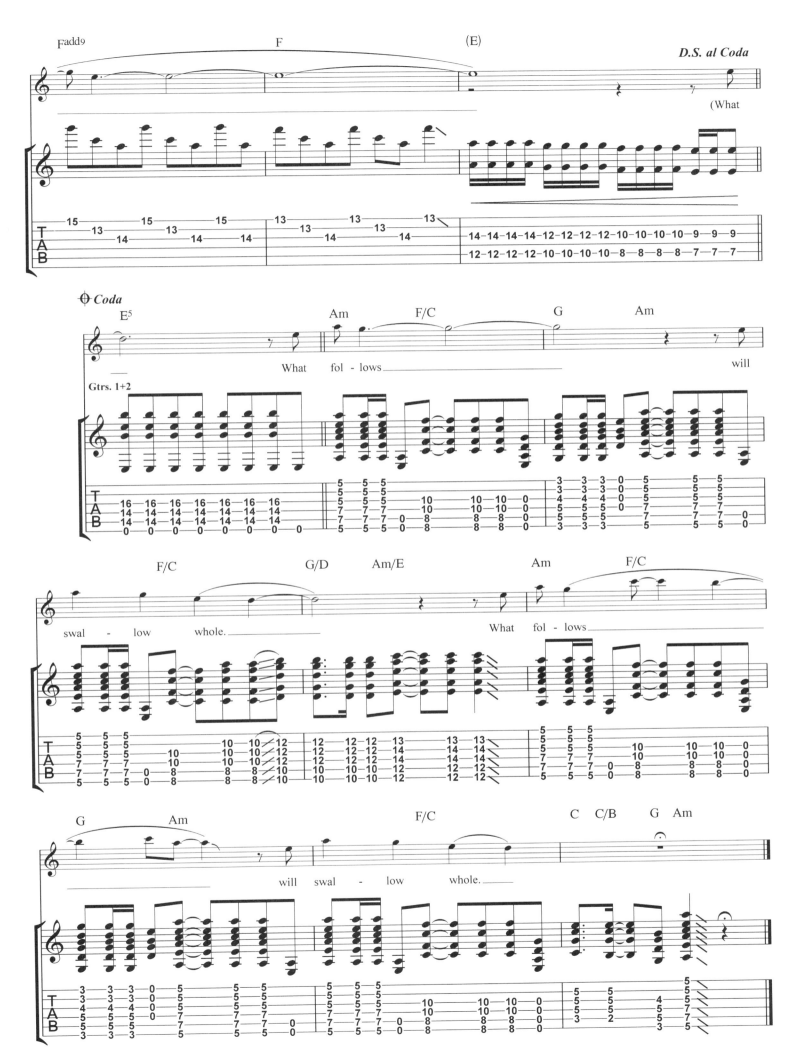

51

FALLING AWAY FROM ME

Words & Music by Korn

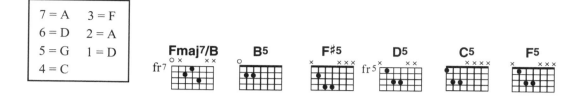

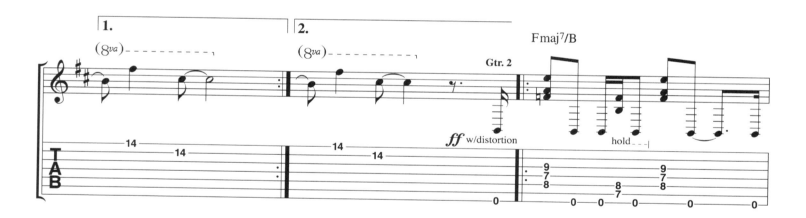

* 7-string guitar. Tune all strings down one tone (7) = A

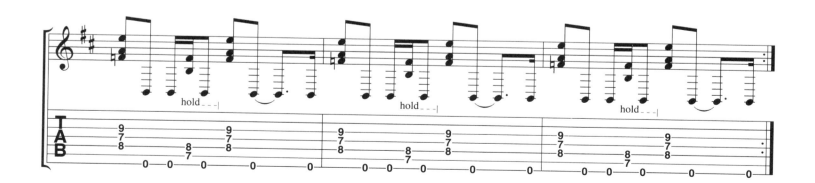

Verse
(B)

1. Hey, I'm feel-ing tired, my time is gone to-day. You're flirt-ing with su-i-cide,
2. Day is here fad-ing, that's when I'm in-sane. I'm flirt-ing with su-i-cide,

Gtr. 1
mf w/clean tone

some-times that's o-kay. Do what oth-ers say, I'm here stand-ing hol-low.
some-times kill the pain. I can't al-ways say, it's gonna be bet-ter to-mor-row.

1.

Fmaj7/B

Fall-ing a-way from me fall-ing a-way from me.

Gtr. 2
ff w/distortion   hold

1. cont.

hold   hold   hold

Fall -ing a - way from me. It's spin - ning round and

round. Fall -ing a - way from me. It's lost and can't be found. Fall -ing a - way from

D. S. al Coda

me. It's spin - ning round and round. Fall -ing a - way from__ me__ slow it down!

I AM HATED

Words & Music by Paul Gray, James Root, Craig Jones, Michael Crahan,
Nathan Jordison, Corey Taylor, Chris Fehn & Mickael Thomson

The whole world is my

* Recorded key Bm, recorded tuning: B F♯ B E G♯ C♯

e-ne-my and I'm a walk-ing tar-get, two times the de-vil with all the sig-ni-fi-cance,

drugged and raped for the love of the mob. I can't stay, be-cause I can't be stopped,

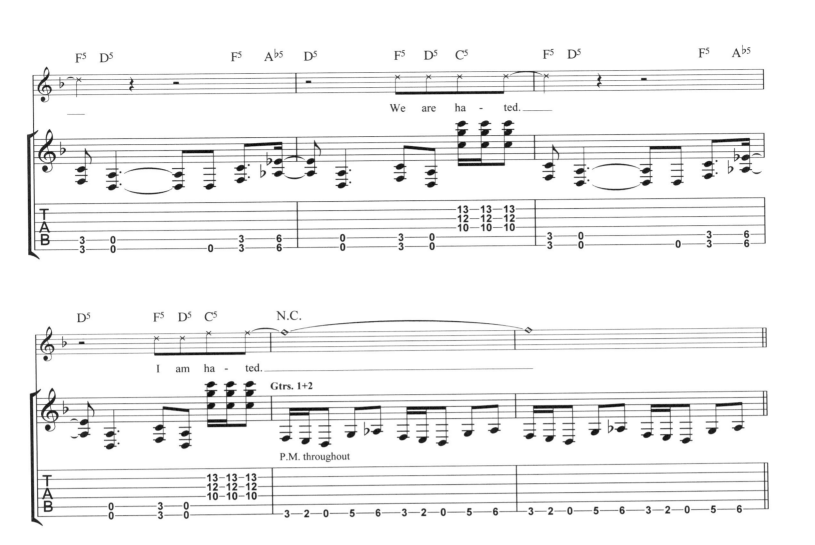

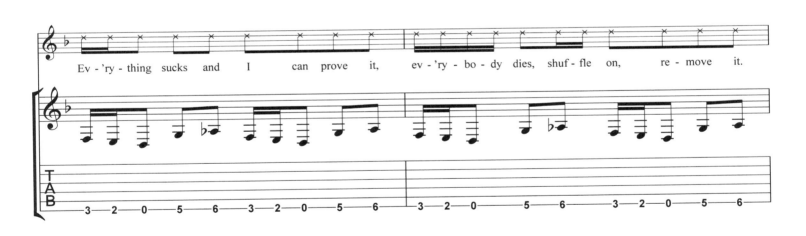

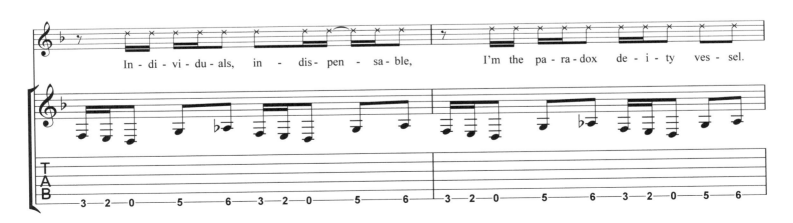

LOW

words & music by Dave Grohl, Taylor Hawkins, Nate Mendel & Chris Shiflett

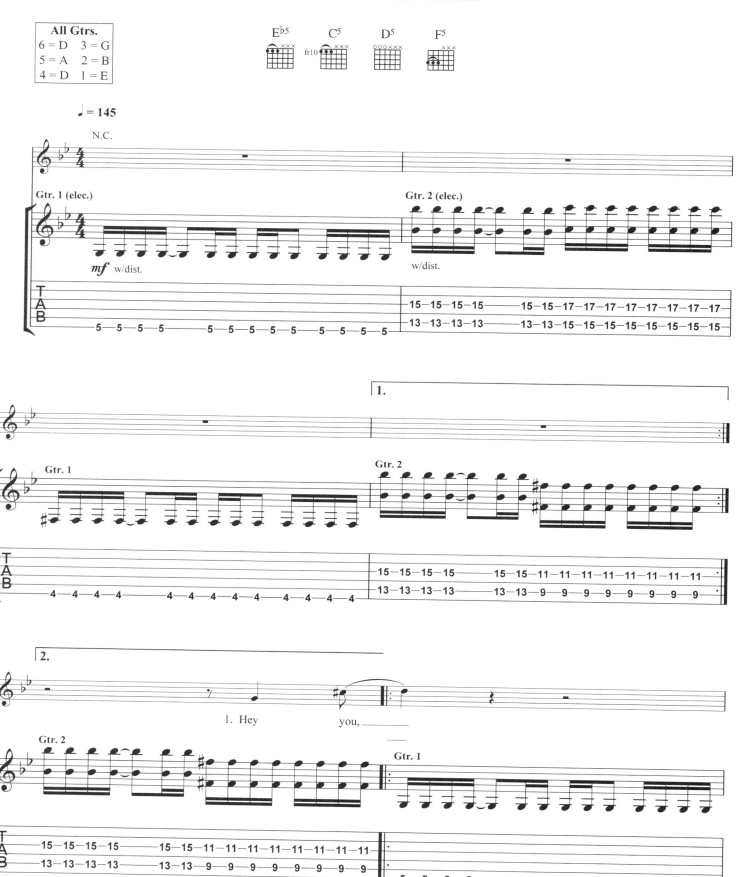

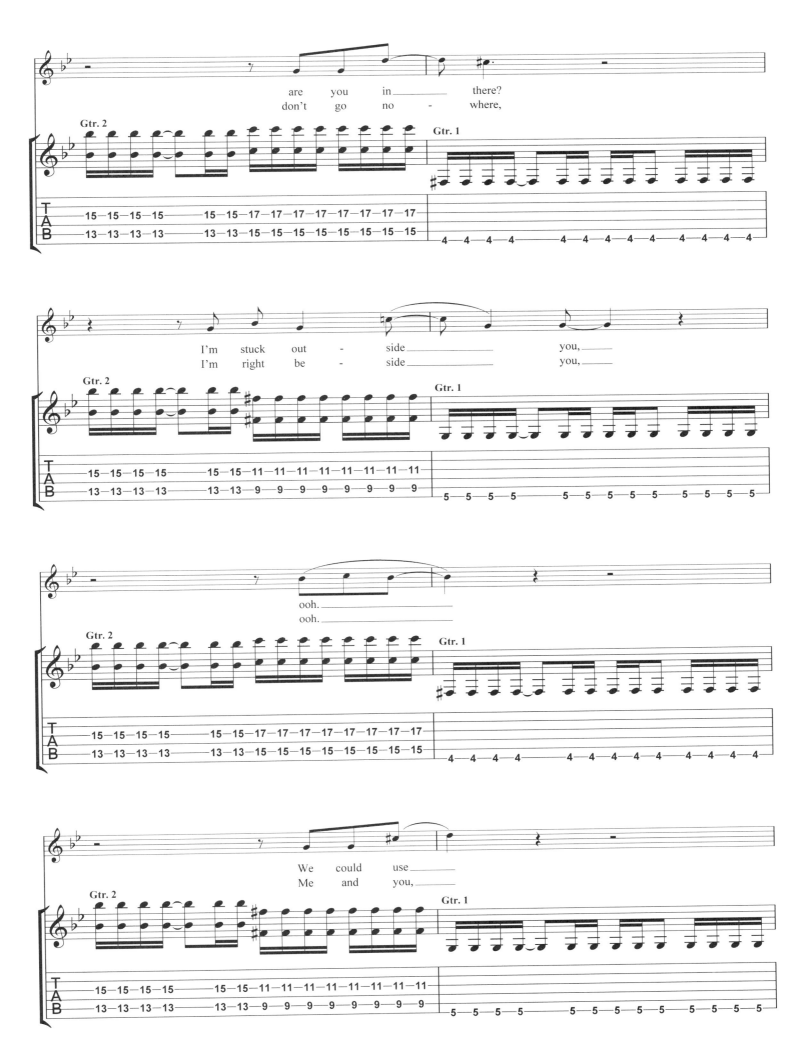

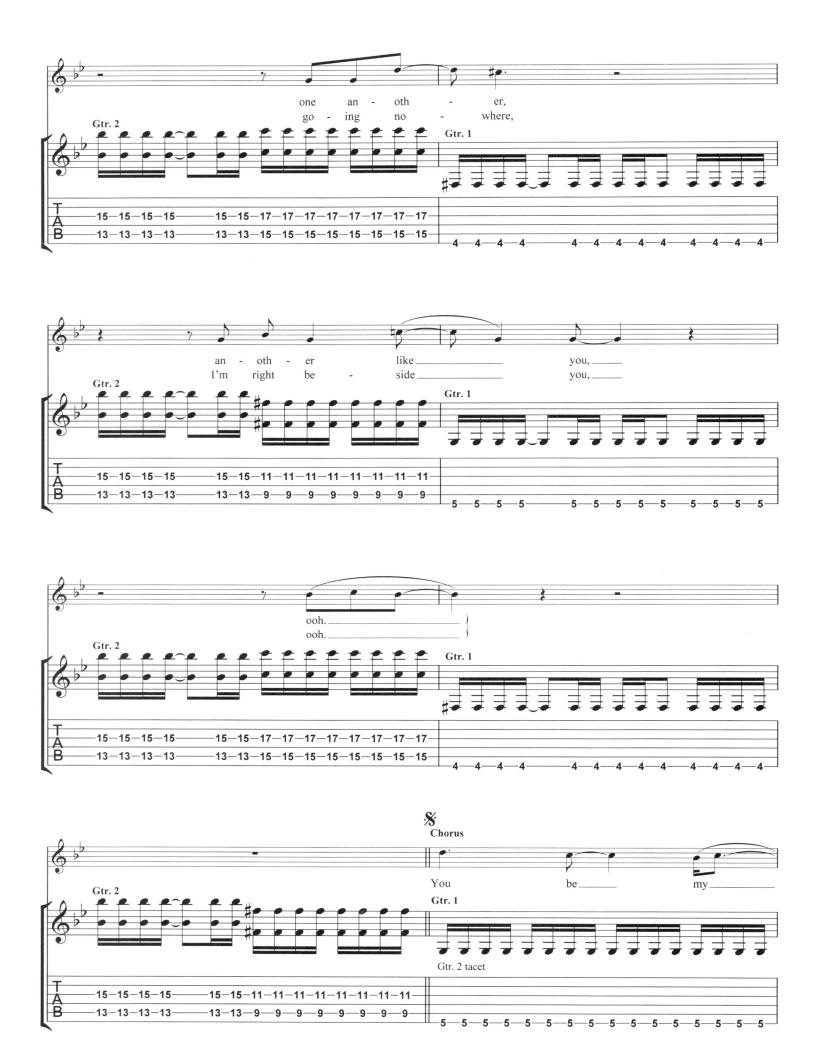

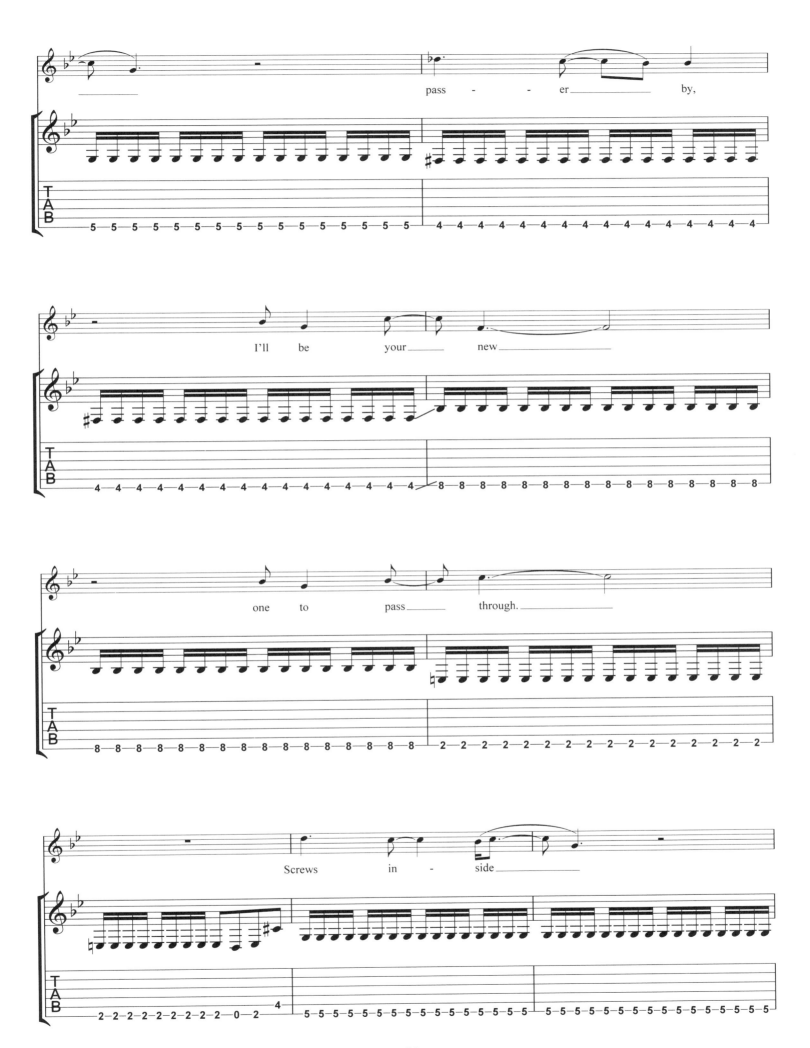

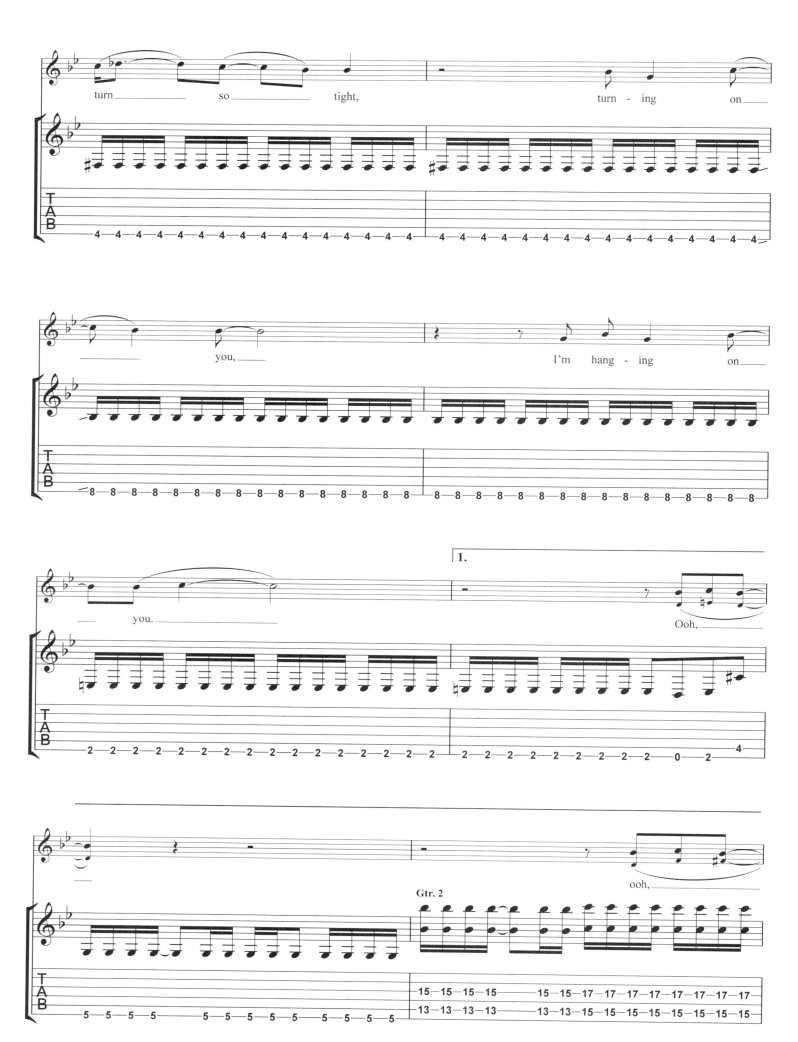

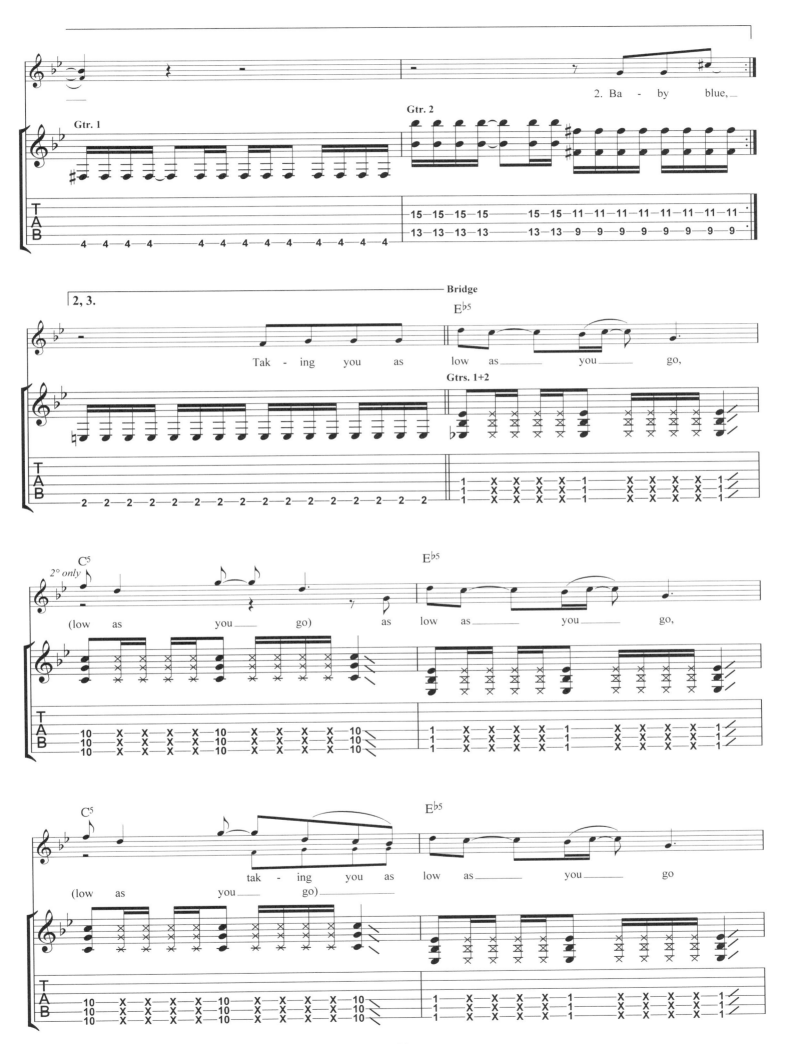

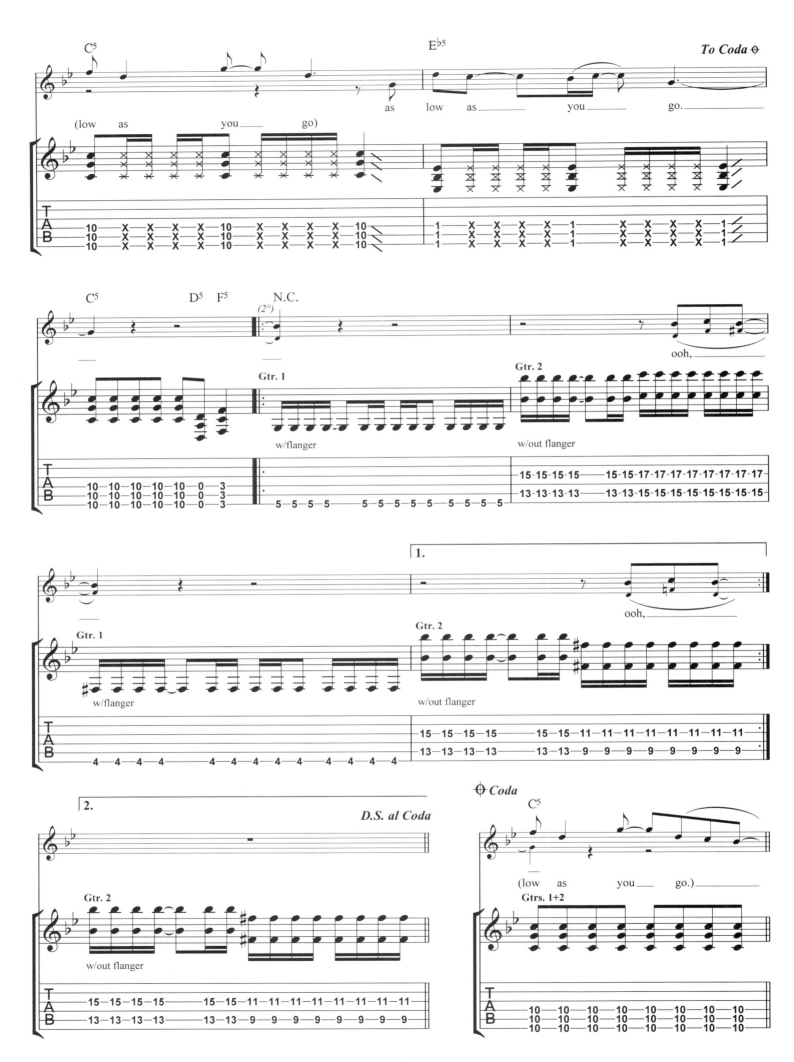

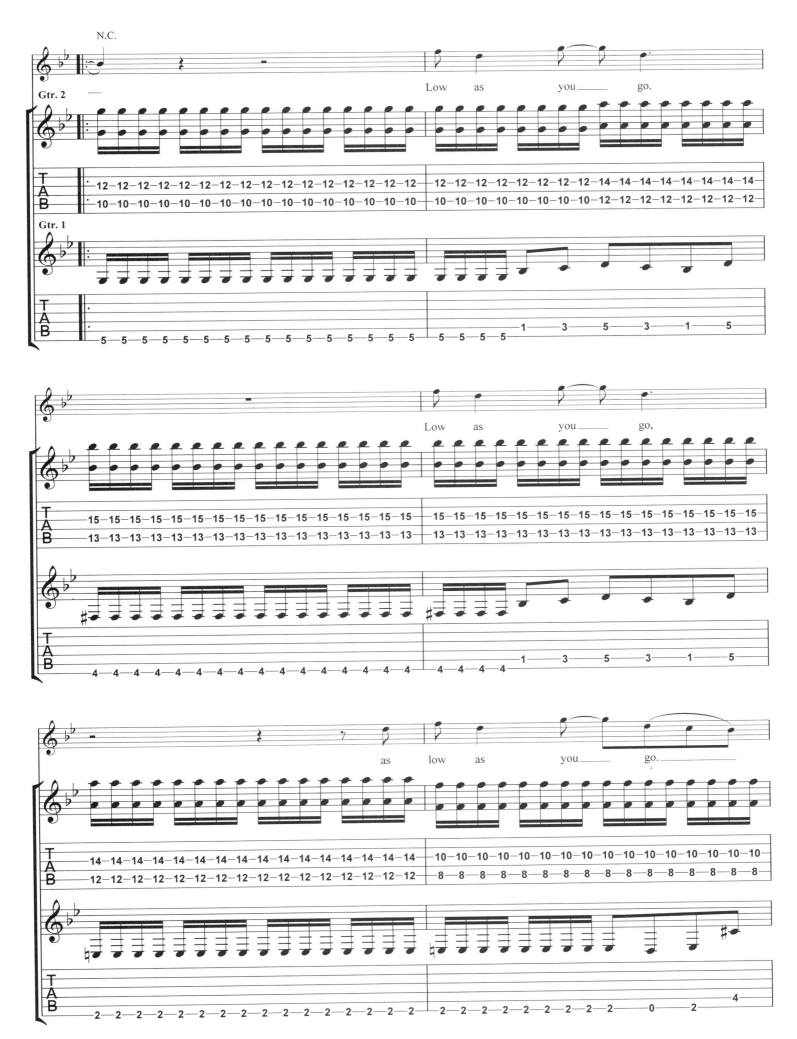

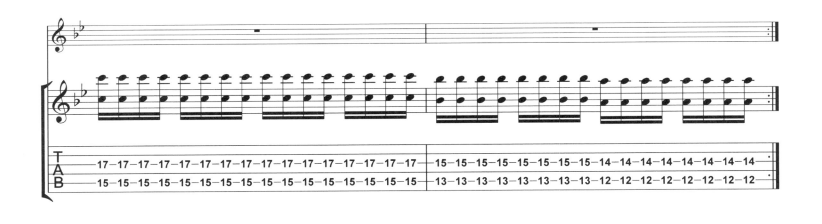

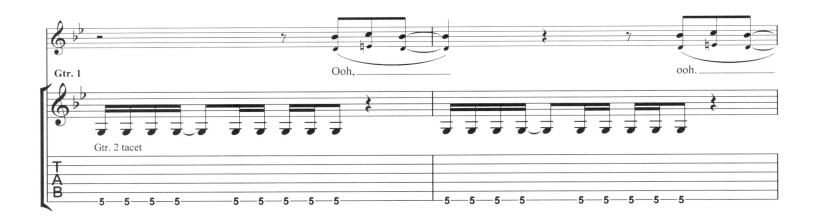

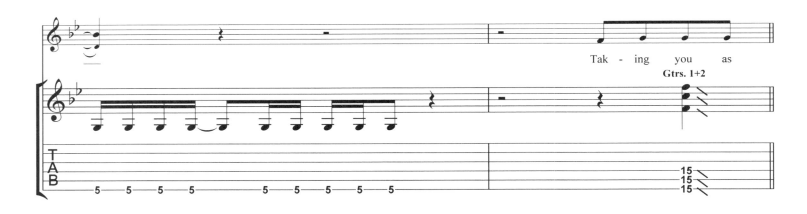

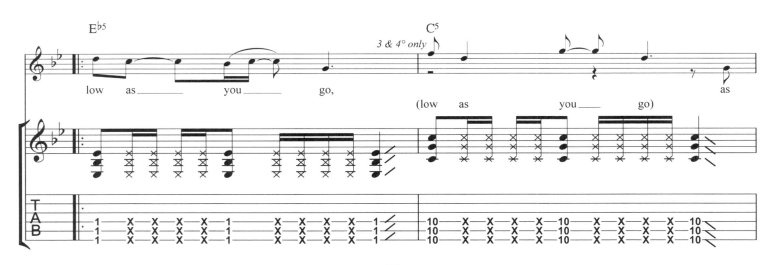

LAST RESORT

Words & Music by Papa Roach

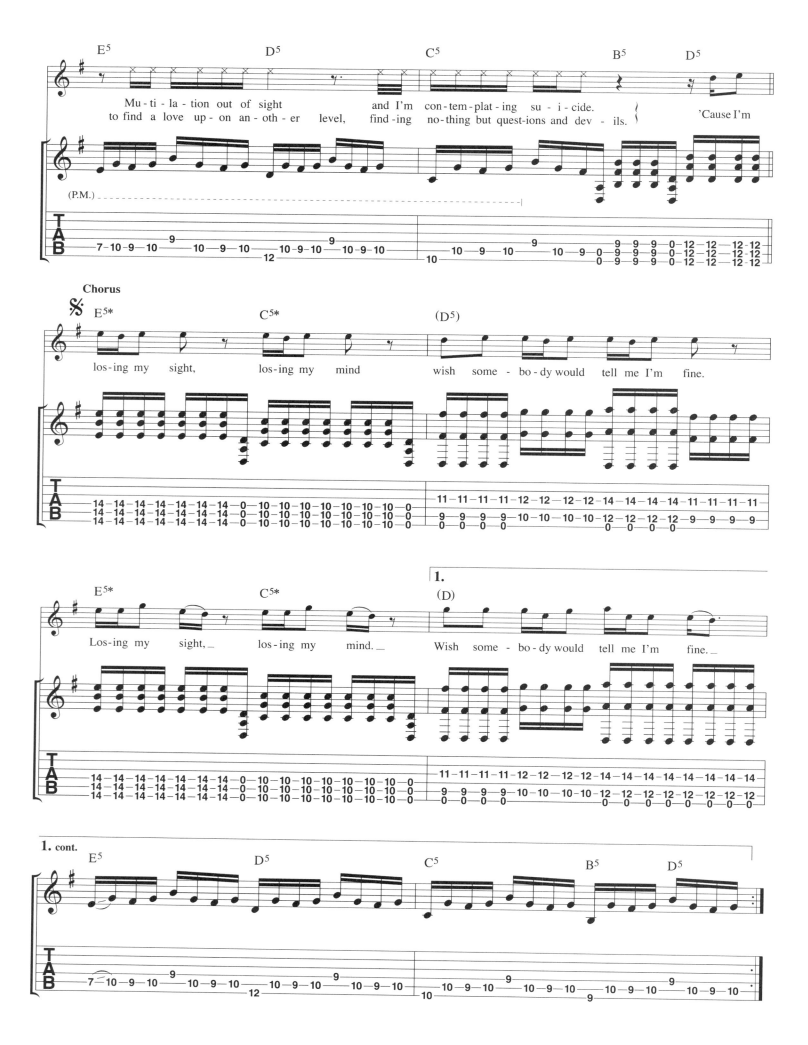

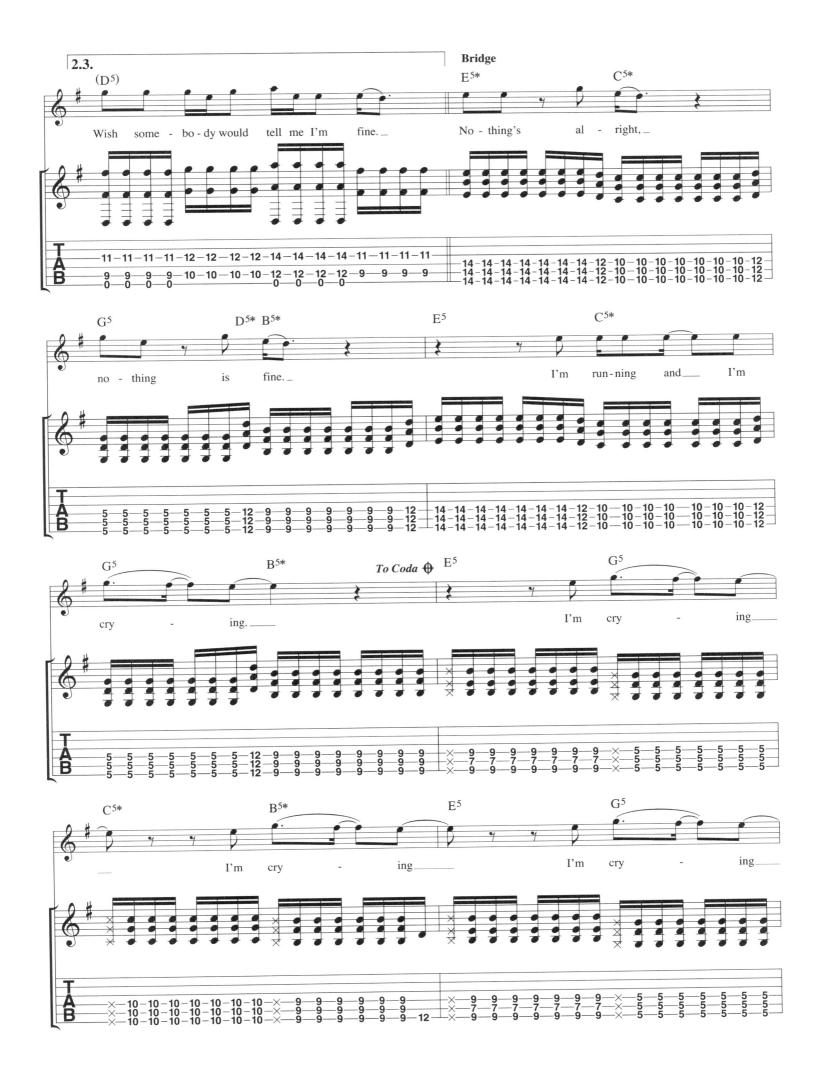

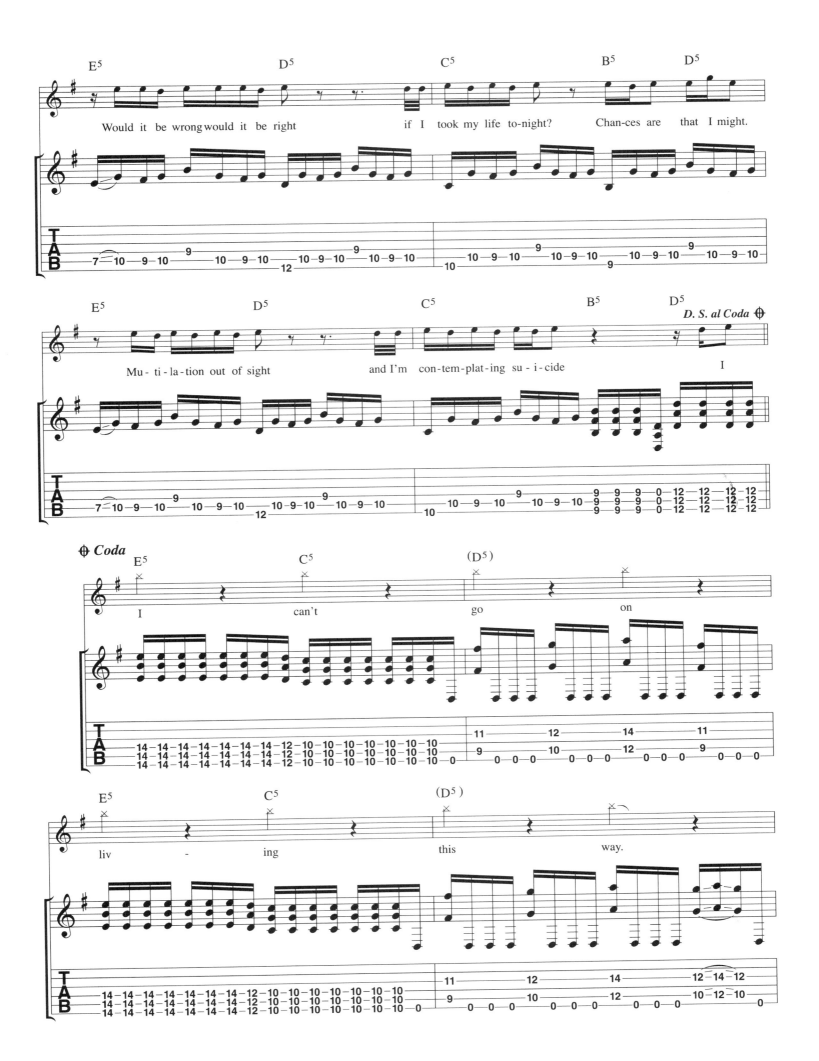

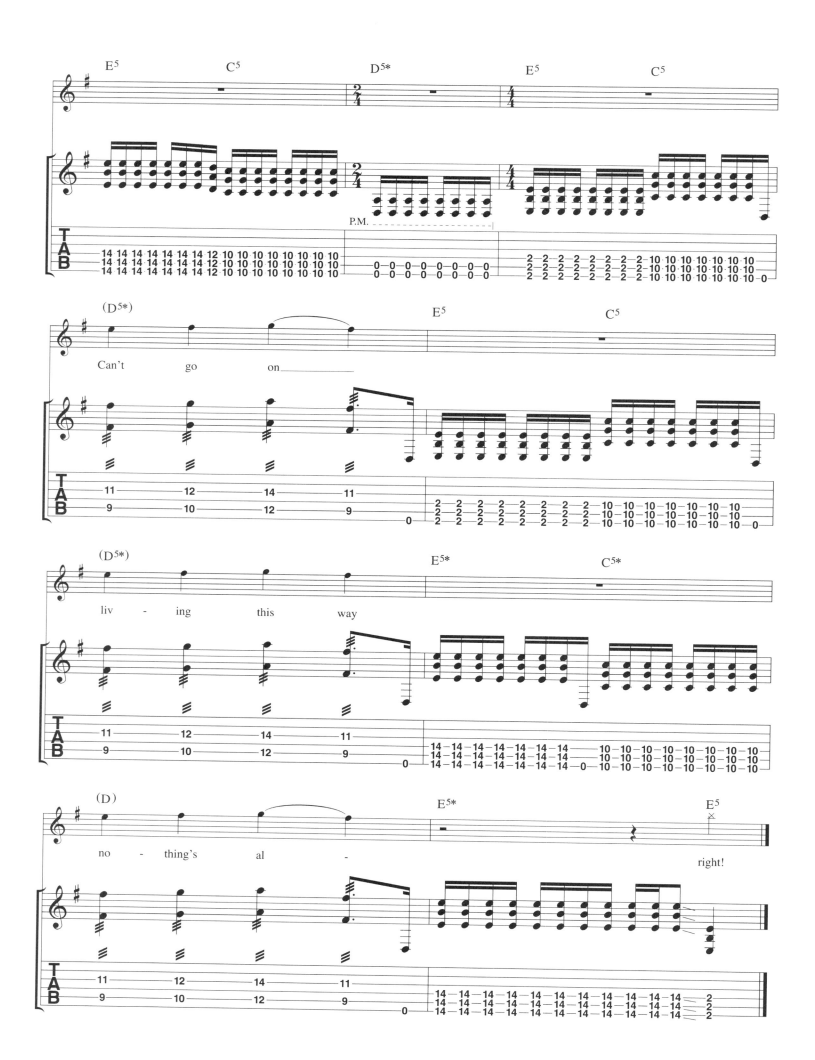

MEIN HERZ BRENNT

Words & Music by Richard Kruspe, Till Lindemann,
Paul Landers, Oliver Riedel, Doktor Lorenz & Christopher Schneider

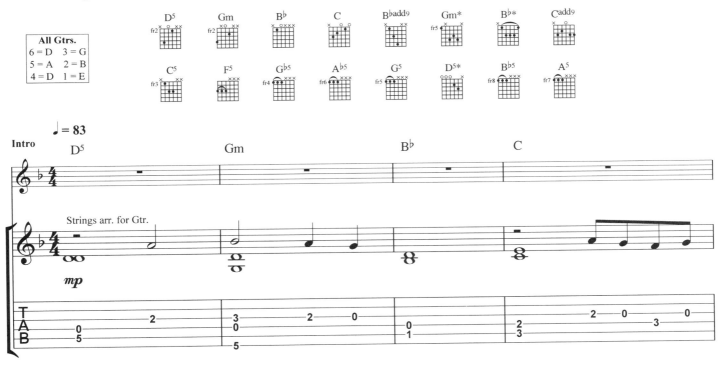

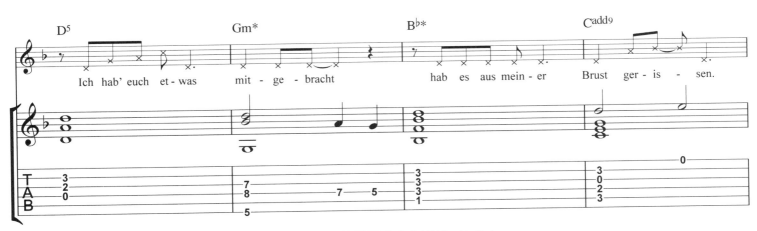

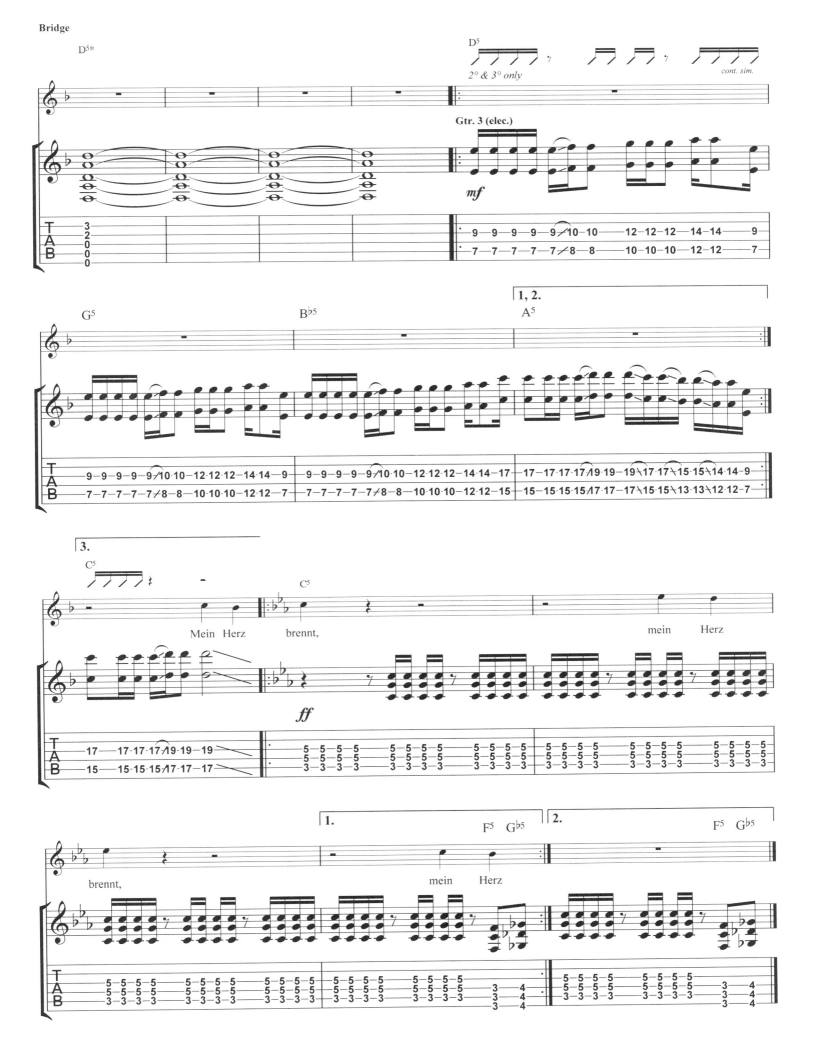

NUMB

Words & Music by Chester Bennington, Mike Shinoda,
Rob Bourdon, Joseph Hahn, Brad Delson & David Farrell

I would be ___ has fall - en a - part ___ right ___ in ___ front ___ of ___ you ___

Pre-chorus

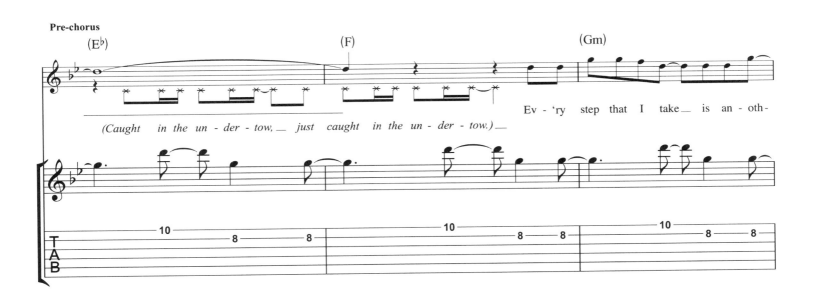

(Caught in the un - der - tow, ___ just caught in the un - der - tow.) ___ Ev - 'ry step that I take ___ is an - oth-

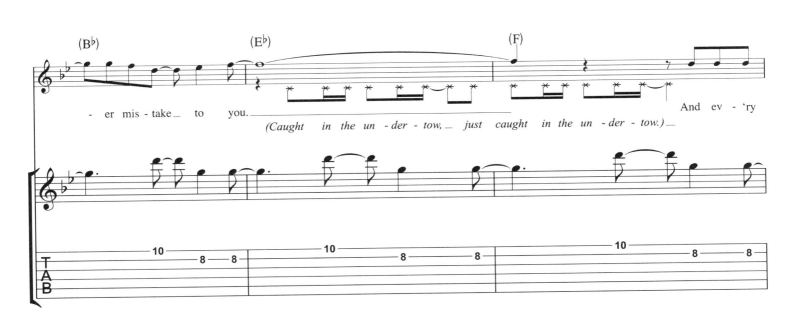

- er mis - take ___ to you. ___ *(Caught in the un - der - tow, ___ just caught in the un - der - tow.)* ___ And ev - 'ry

RIGHT HERE IN MY ARMS

words & music by Ville Valo, Mikko Lindstroem,
Mika Karpinnen, Mikko Paananen & Jussi Salminen

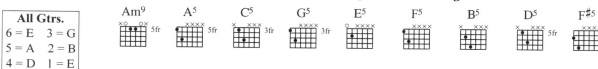

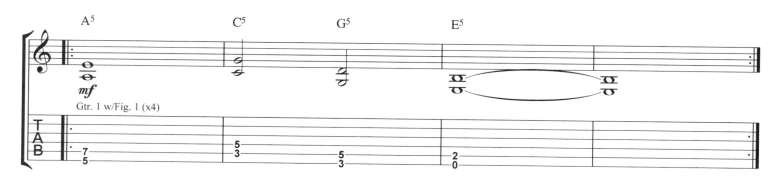

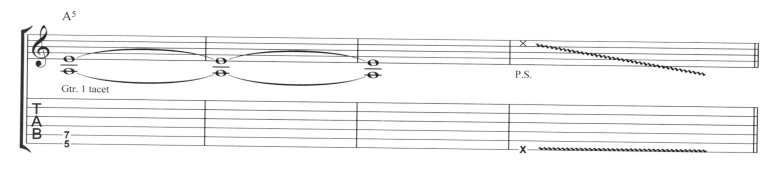

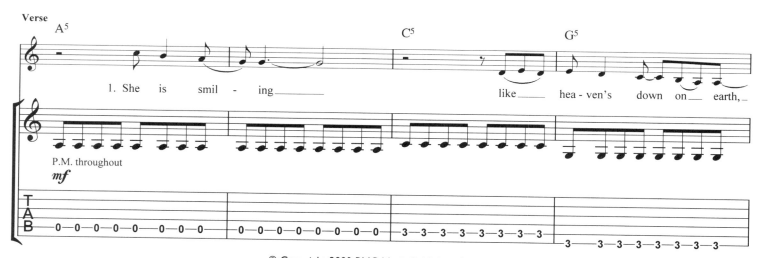

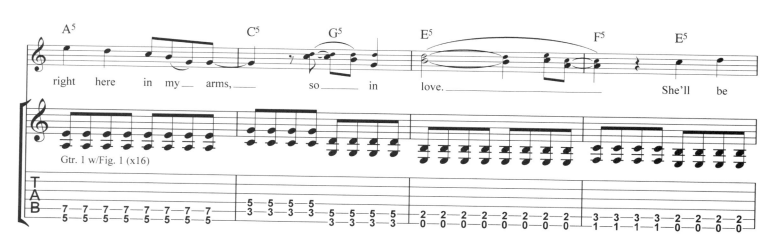

Freely, not picked.

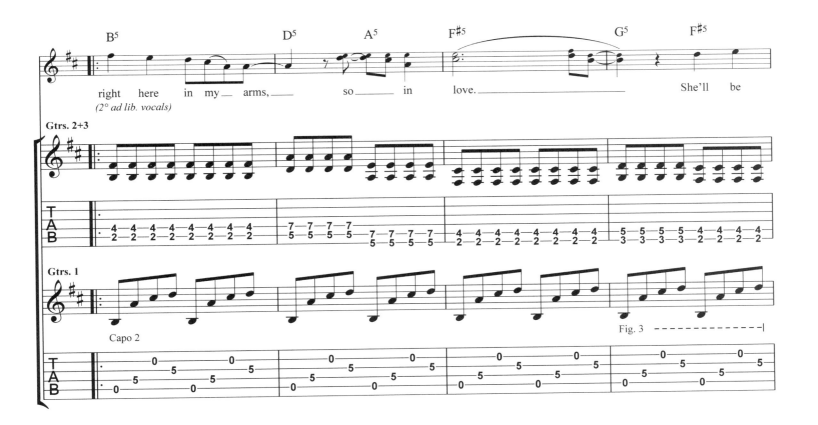

PARTY HARD

words & music by Andrew W.K.

SLITHER

words & music by Matt Sorum, Duff 'Rose' McKagan,
David Kushner, Saul Hudson & Scott Weiland

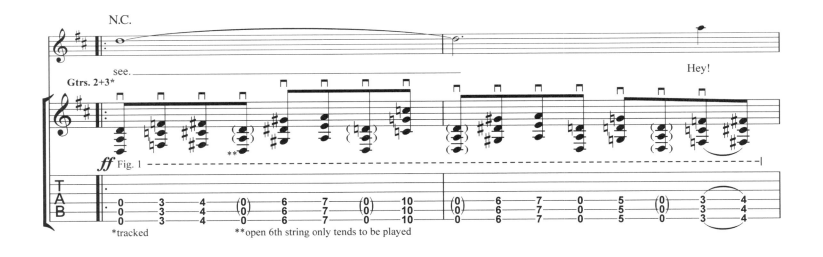

N.C.

see.

Hey!

Gtrs. 2+3*

ff Fig. 1

*tracked   **open 6th string only tends to be played

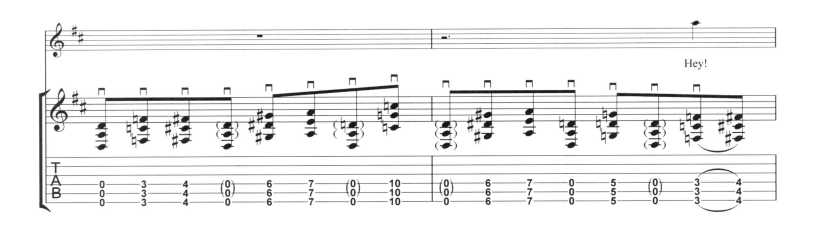

Hey!

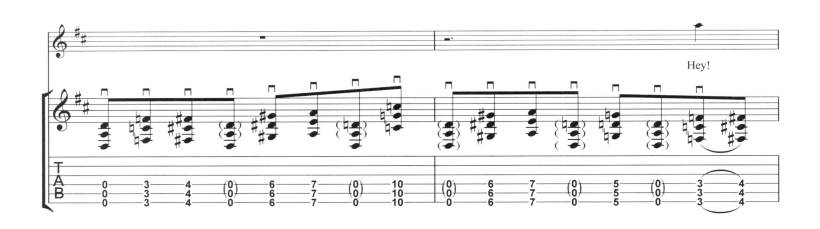

Hey!

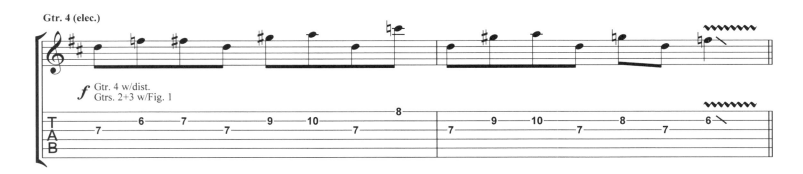

Gtr. 4 (elec.)

f Gtr. 4 w/dist.
Gtrs. 2+3 w/Fig. 1

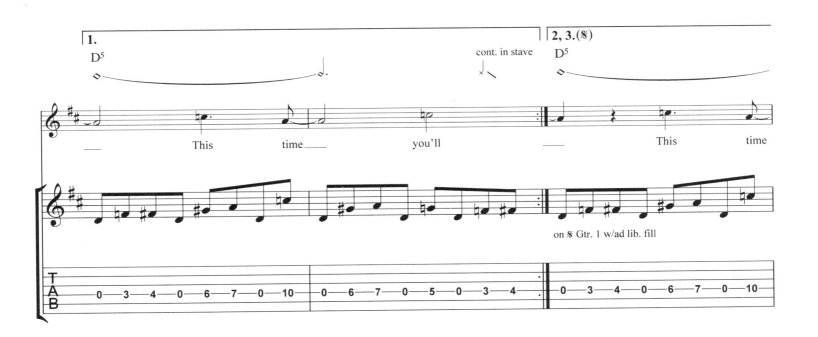

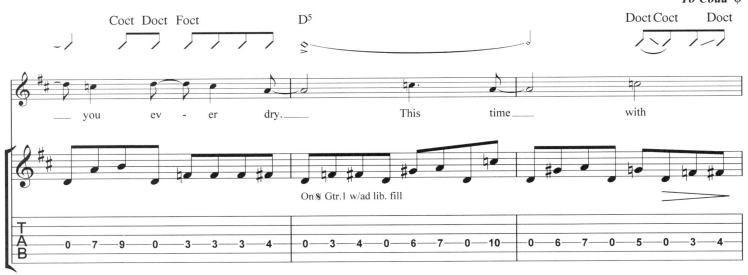

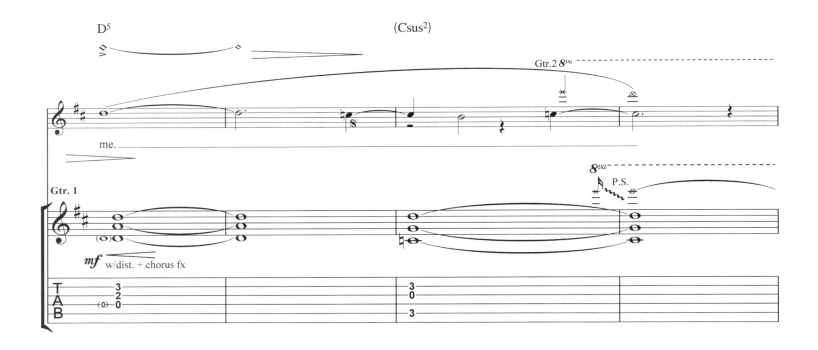

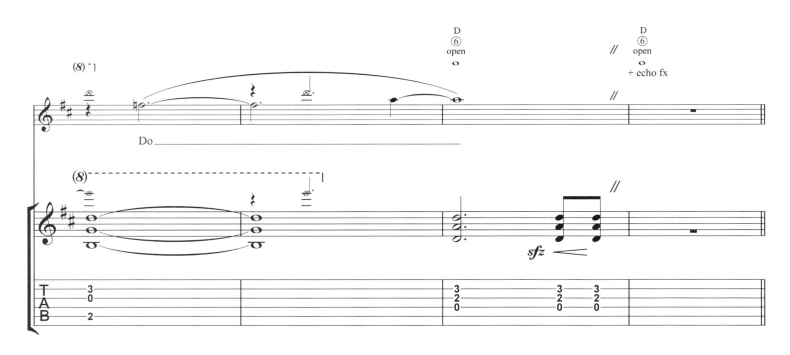

III

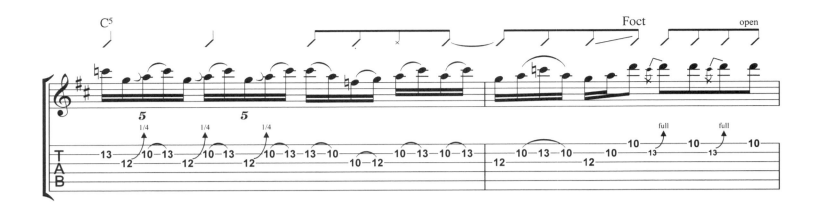

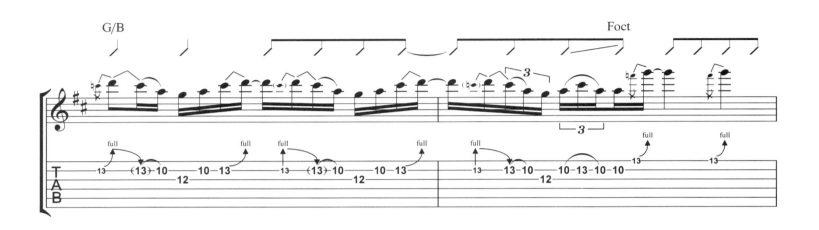

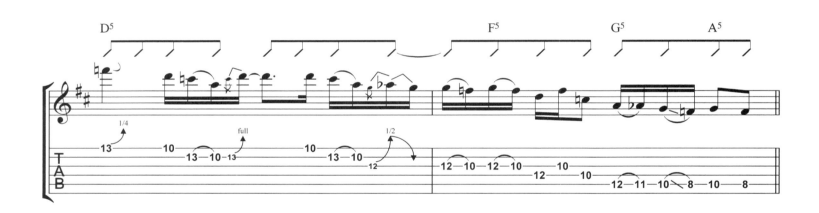

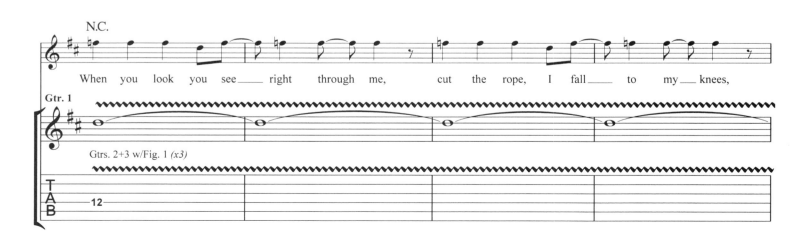

When you look you see___ right through me, cut the rope, I fall___ to my___ knees,

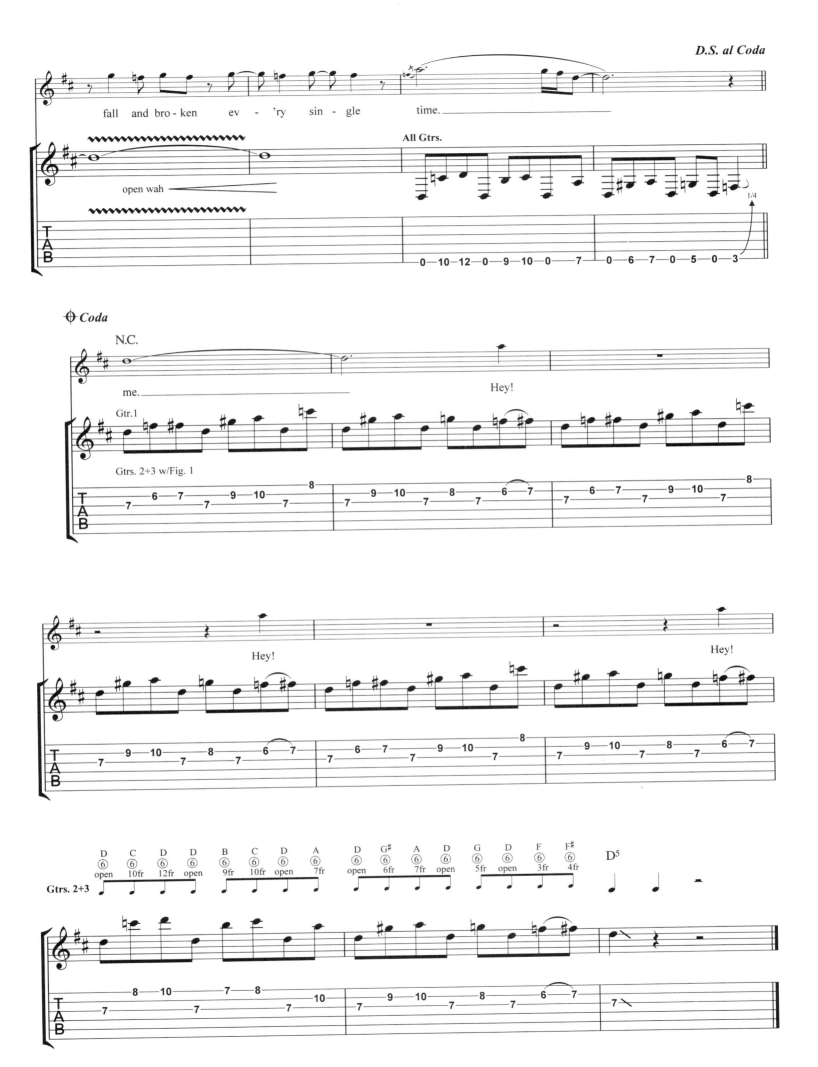

TAKE A LOOK AROUND
(THEME FROM "M:I-2")

Words by Fred Durst
Music by Lalo Schifrin

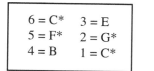

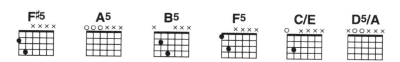

good comes the bad, the bad comes the good. But
where you gon-na run when you star-ing down the ca-ble of my

I'm a live my life like I should.
mic? Point-ed at your grill like a gun.

Now all the cri-tics wan-na hit it, this hit can
Limp Biz-kit is rock in' the set it's like

how we do it, just be cause they don't get it. But
Rus - sian roul - ette when you're plac-ing your bet. So-

I'll stay fit - ted, new e - ra com - mit - ted.
don't be up - set when you're broke and you're done 'cause

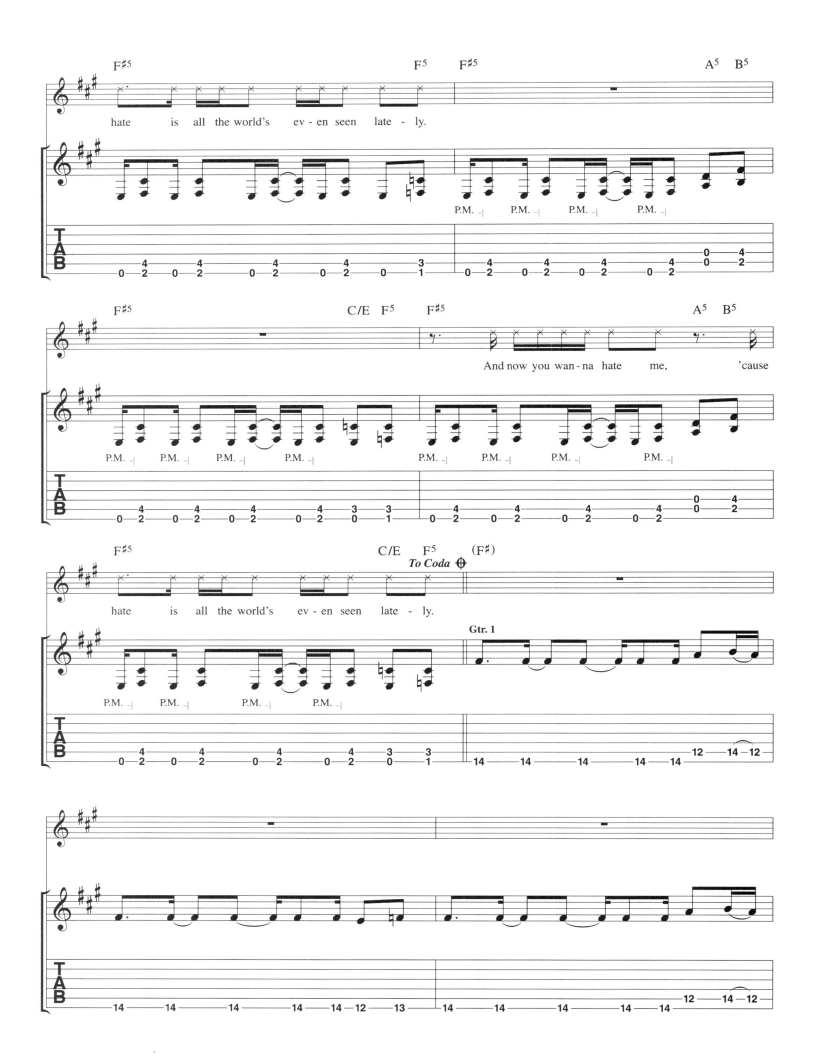

beat - ing up my mind ev - 'ry se - cond with my fist.

And ev - 'ry - bo - dy wan - na run, ev - 'ry - bo - dy wan - na hide from the gun.

You can take a ride through this life if you want but you can't take the edge off the knife no sir!

And now you want your mon - ey back, but you're de - nied but your brain's fried from the sack.

WAKE UP

words by Zack de la Rocha
Music by Rage Against the Machine

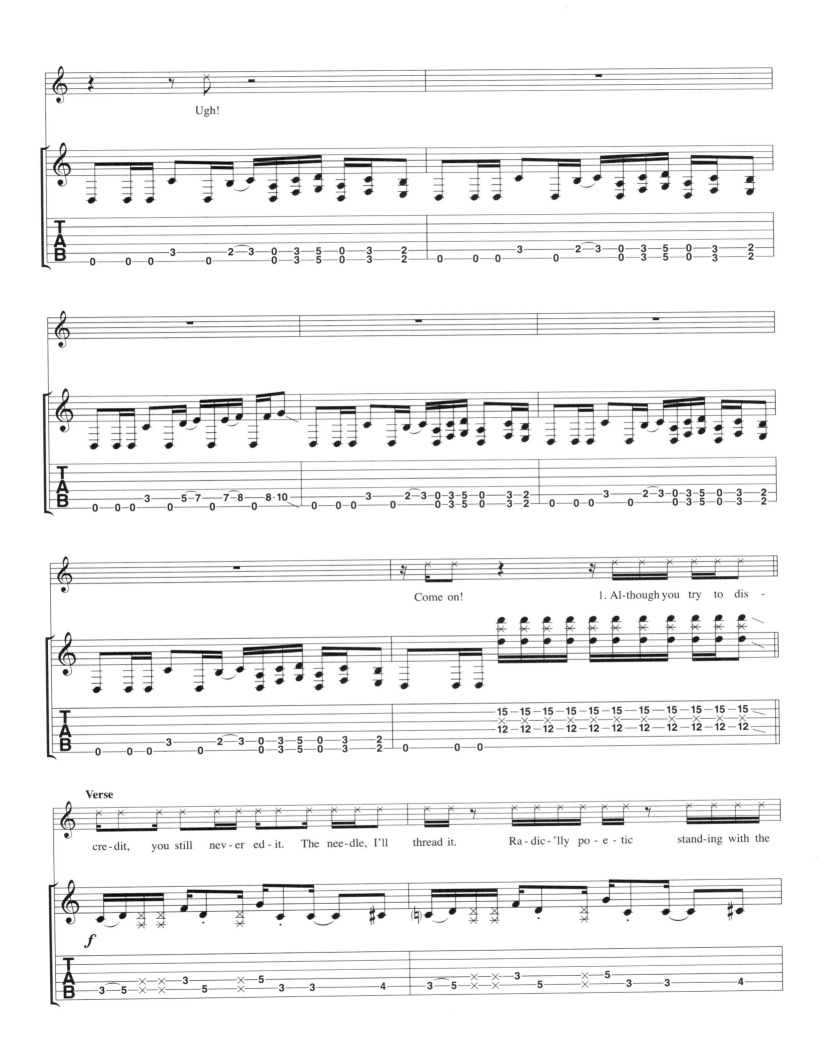

fu-ry that they had in six - ty six and like E - dou-ble I'm mad__ still knee-deep in the sys - tem's shit.

Hoo-ver, he was a bo-dy re-mov-er, I'll give you a dose,__ but it will nev-er come close__ to the rage

built up in - side of me, fist in the air in the land of hy - po - cri - sy.

2. Move - ments come and move - ments go, lead-ers speak, move-ments cease when their heads are down.__

'Cause all these punks got bul-lets in their heads. De - part-ment of po-lice, the jud - ges, the Feds,

net-works at work keep-in' peo-ple calm. You know they went af-ter King when he spoke out on Vi - et-nam,

he turned the po - wer to the have - nots, and then came the___ shot.

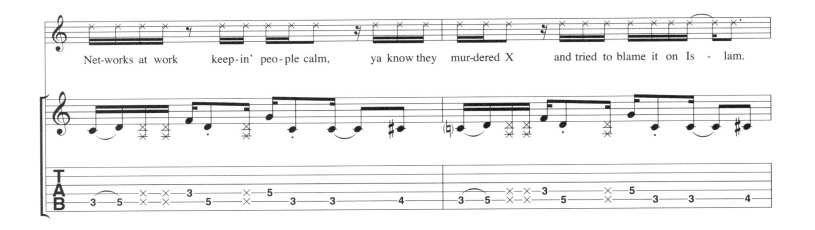

Net-works at work   keep-in' peo-ple calm,   ya know they mur-dered X   and tried to blame it on Is - lam.

He turned the pow-er to the have - nots   and then came the____ shot.

w/talk box

Solo

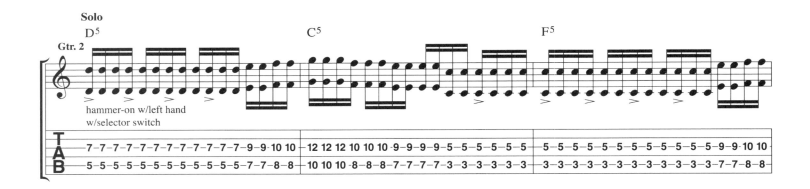

hammer-on w/left hand
w/selector switch

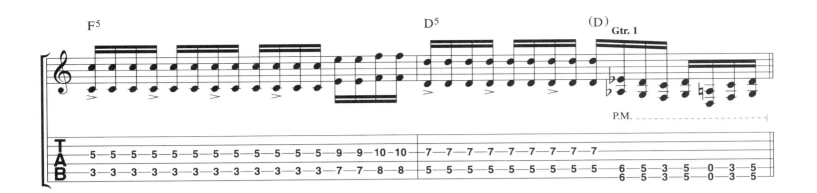

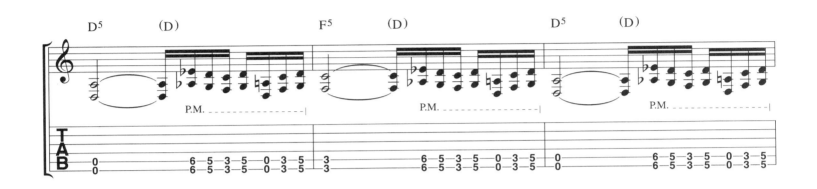

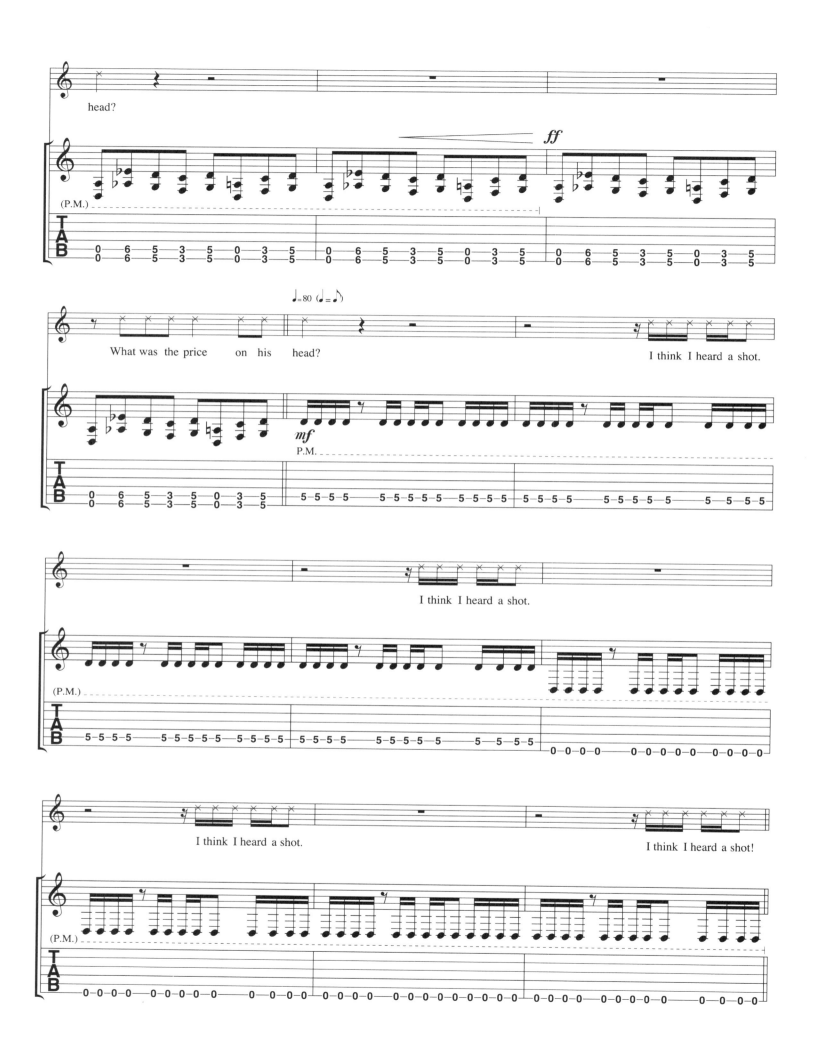

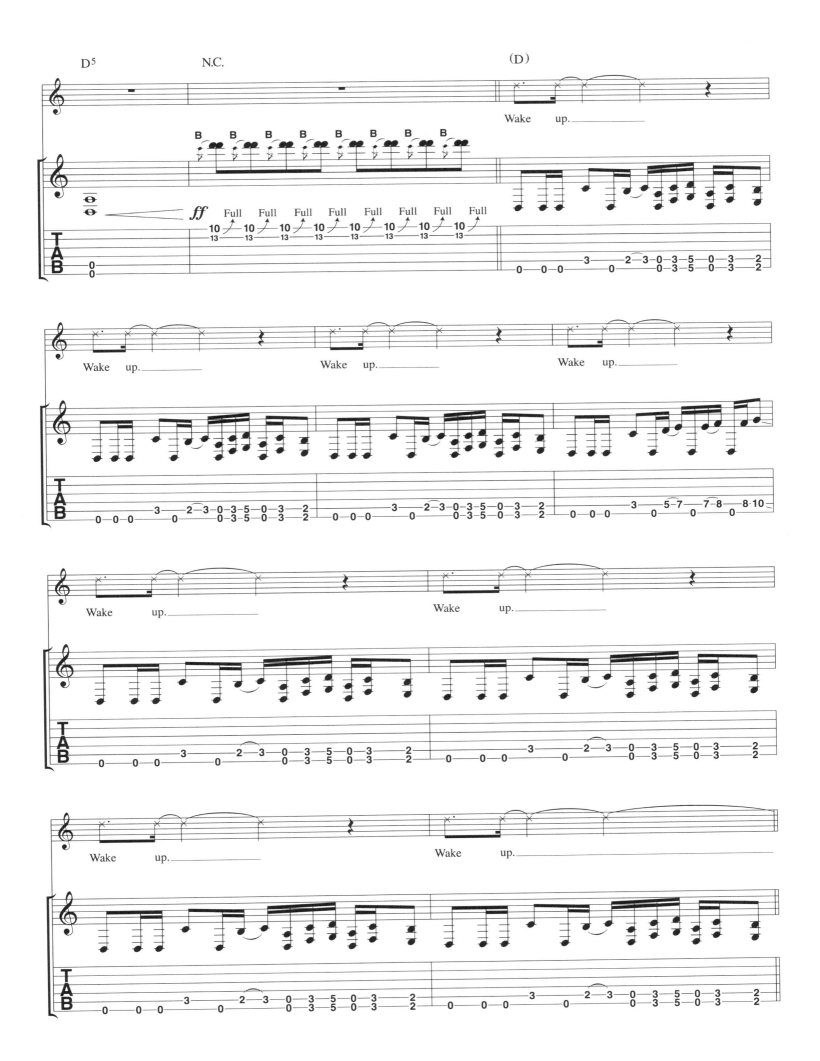

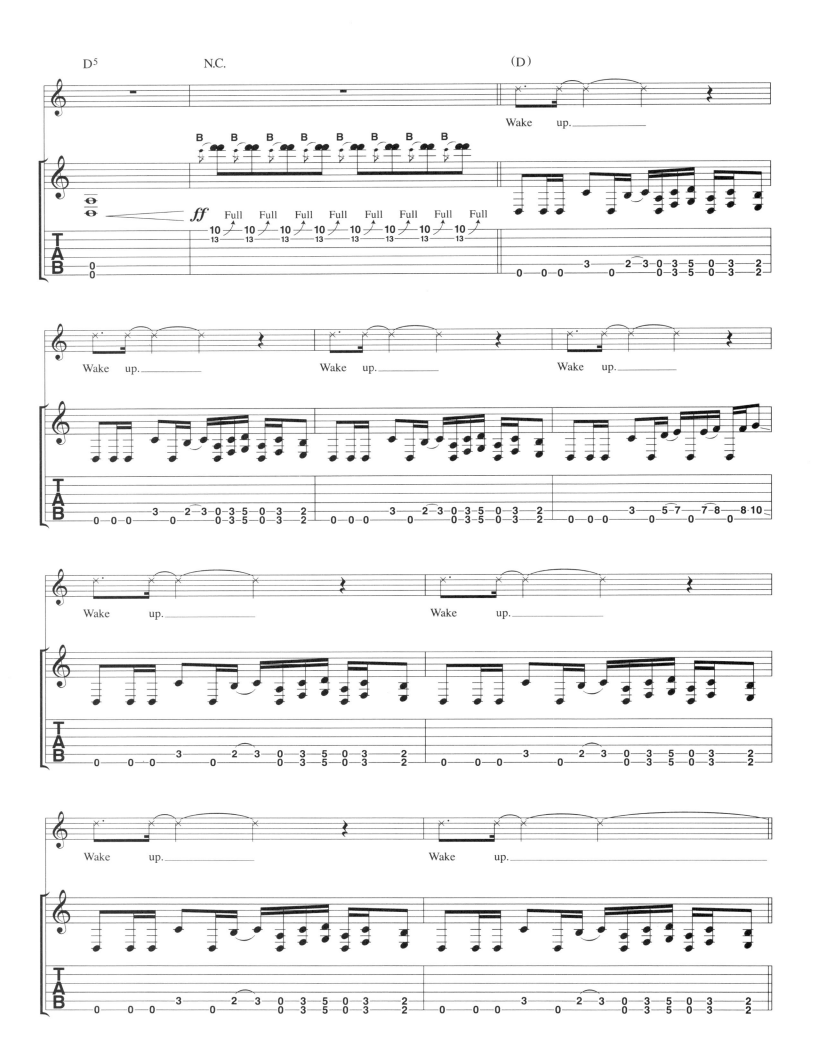

The essential NÜ METAL playlist